Landmark Visit

CW00556649

→ Bl

29. JAN 11,

11.

20. DEC 08

Received to
03/01/09 .

29/1/09
03. OCT 09,

13. OCT 09.

09. 10

5 027646 000

Bl

This book may be returned to any Wiltshire
library. To renew this book phone your library
or visit the website: www.wiltshire.gov.uk

Wiltshire
COUNTY COUNCIL

LM6.108.5

Published by
Landmark Publishing
Ashbourne Hall, Cokayne Ave, Ashbourne,
Derbyshire DE6 1EJ England

Published in the UK by
Landmark Publishing Ltd,
Ashbourne Hall, Cokayne Ave, Ashbourne, Derbyshire DE6 1EJ England
☎ (01335) 347349 Fax: (01335) 347303 e-mail: landmark@clara.net

1st Edition
ISBN: 978 184306 384 1

Front cover: Sign Post outside York Mansion House

Back cover, top: Whitby Steps

Back cover, second down: St Nic's Market, Bristol (© Destination Bristol)

Back cover, third down: Kings College, Cambridge

Back cover, bottom: Gateshead Millennium Bridge & Tyme Bridge, Newcastle

Back cover, right: Churnet Valley, Ashbourne

England

SCOTLAND

0 20 40miles

0 1 2kms

N
W   E
S

○ Berwick upon Tweed

○ Alnwick

○ Carlisle   ○
Newcastle upon Tyne
                ○ Durham

        ○ Barnard Castle   ○ Whitby

○ Windermere   North Sea

        ○ Harrogate
LANCASTER ○ Skipton   ○ York
        ○ LEEDS   ○ Beverley

Liverpool ○ Manchester   ENGLAND
    ○   SHEFFIELD
    ○ Chester ○ Lincoln

        ○ Ashbourne   Boston ○   ○ Cromer
                              ○ Kings Lynn
                      ○ Stamford   ○ Norwich

        ○ Much Wenlock
○ Ludlow   ○ BIRMINGHAM   Bury St Edmunds
                                      ○
WALES Worcester ○ Stratford   ○ Cambridge ○ Ipswich
                    on Avon

Irish Sea

        ○ Gloucester
                ○ Oxford
    Bristol
    ○   ○ Windsor
    ○ Bath   ○ Rochester
    ○ Wells   LONDON
                    ○ Canterbury

○ Taunton ○ Salisbury ○ Winchester
                        ○ Arundel

    ○ Exeter ○ Lyme Regis

○ Truro ○ Plymouth   English Channel

Contents

Whitby Abbey

Short Breaks in England

Short Breaks in England aims to give you the basic information you are likely to need in order to compare suggested locations for a short break. This guide is not an accommodation guide, it's full of practical information about each town or city I have selected. Where possible I have included web site details that you should be able to follow up for a more thorough understanding of what is on offer. In this day and age there is a plethora of information available to consumers but our main consideration in putting this guide book together was to produce a single source to help you to compare different places and explore somewhere new.

I have included brief descriptions of how to get to locations if you decide to leave your car behind, although some are easier to get to than others by public transport! You will find little tasters of what there is to see and do within walking distance of the centre and then some interesting or important attractions further afield; generally these are within 30 minutes drive time from the town or featured city. Some places are recommended as a centre for your stay and have plenty to offer for a long weekend. Others are more of a hub, with trips out to various attractions.

If you want to treat yourself I have listed a couple of choice hotels and restaurants, with web site details where available. In some cases there are quite a few to chose from and these are really tasters to give you a feel for what is on offer. As with all such recommendations please bear in mind that they are subjective and may change,

Kayaker on Lake Windermere

The Cathedral and Castle Square, Lincoln

Landmark Trust

The Landmark Trust is a charity established in 1965 to prevent the loss or irreversible alteration of small but worthwhile buildings of architectural or historical significance. The restored buildings are let as quality holiday accommodation (self catering) to cover on-going maintenance etc. The Landmark Trust has almost 200 properties in its portfolio. Listed are properties within 15 miles of the towns and cities listed in this guide. I suggest you visit the Trust's website where you will be able to find details of the properties and how to make a booking, alternatively:

Booking office:

☎ 01628 825925

email: bookings@ landmarktrust.org.uk

www.landmarktrust.org.uk

Knaresborough, Harrogate

sometimes very rapidly. If you are able to let us know if things have changed please do, it will help with future editions of this guide.

You will notice that in quite a few locations I have featured properties operated by the Landmark Trust. There is no connection between the Trust and Landmark Publishing, but I felt that their properties had so much to offer. They are a charitable trust pre-serving properties which might otherwise have been lost.

England has so much to offer with such varied countryside and cities steeped in heritage, . I think this guide gives both a flavour of that and the opportunity to enjoy areas with which you may not be already acquainted. I do hope this guide will help you select new places to visit and provide you with lots of good reasons for getting away.

Public Transport

For practical travel comparisons, Transport Direct website is a useful single source for comparing road, rail and coach/bus options. www.transportdirect.info

There are numerous websites offering tickets for travel by rail or coach/bus (I mention buses because in some cases it may be necessary to complete a journey using the local bus service).

Cath Walton

Old boat hoist, Plymouth

Harbour, Bristol

Farmers' Market, Taunton

Sunset over Whitby Bay

Left Top: Lendal Bridge over the River Ouse, York

Middle: Stratford-upon-Avon Canal, near Lapworth locks

Left Bottom: Bath

Lake Windermere

Useful Contacts

National Trust (NT):
www.nationaltrust.org.uk

English Heritage (EH):
www.english-heritage.org.uk

National Express:
www.nationalexpress.com

Stagecoach:
www.stagecoachbus.com

Train Enquiries:
www.nationalrail.co.uk

www.thetrainline.com

Transport Direct:
www.transportdirect.info

Howick Hall Gardens

Getting There

By Road

The A1 north of Newcastle upon Tyne passes Alnwick.

By Rail & Bus

Nearest station at Alnmouth (2.5 miles/4km).

There are coach/bus services to Alnwick from around the country although you may have to make changes to complete the journey.

Background Briefing

This impressive stone-built town, with its dignified cobbled streets and alleyways, makes a pleasant base for a weekend break. It sits on the gently rising ground overlooking the valley of the River Aln. The recently refurbished market place conveys the atmosphere of a medieval market town and is the centre for many local events including Farmers' Markets, Food Festivals and an International Music Festival. Enjoy shows at the Alnwick Playhouse, see an exhibition at the Bondgate Gallery, try hands-on activities at the Bailiffgate Museum or visit the new Willowburn Leisure Centre with its children's pool, health suite and gym. The mighty medieval fortress of Alnwick Castle dominates the town. It is one of Europe's finest and a major tourist attraction.

Places to Visit

Alnwick Castle
NE66 1NQ
☎ 01665 510777
www.alnwickcastle.com

The Alnwick Garden
Denwick Lane, NE66 1YU
☎ 01665 511350
www.alnwickgarden.com
Alnwick Castle is the second largest inhabited castle in England, since 1309 home to the Percy family (now Dukes of Northumberland). Hotspur was a son of the First Earl of Northumberland, killed at Shrewsbury in 1403 fighting Henry IV. Parts of the castle were used in the first two Harry Potter movies. The Duchess's recently completed £9 million garden is an impressive attraction alongside this stunning castle and the adjacent Hulme Park, which extends to 3,000 acres of outstanding parkland.

Bailiffgate Museum
14 Bailiffgate, Alnwick,
NE66 1LX
☎ 01665 605847
The people of north Northumberland depicted in lively, interactive style through an exploration of six engaging themes.

Hulme Park
Ratten Row, Alnwick, NE66 1NQ
☎ 01665 510777
Hulme Park adjoins the castle; there are 3,000 acres of outstanding parkland, enclosed by a nine mile long wall. Admission is free but check for opening times. Within the park are the remains of a 13th century Carmelite priory and Brizlee Tower, an 18th century folly tower.

Attractions Nearby

Dunstanburgh Castle (EH)
(8miles/13km)
Craster, NE66 3TT
☎ 01665 576231
This once-grand fortification is now a ruin which dominates this stretch of Northumberland's coastline.

Cragside (NT)

(10 miles/16km)
Rothbury, Morpeth, NE65 7PX
☎ 01669 620333
This Victorian mansion, designed by Richard Norman Shaw, was the first house in the world to be lit by hydroelectric power. Large rock garden and woodland estate, which is one of the red squirrel's last strongholds. Children can explore a tricky rhododendron maze and an adventure playground.

Bamburgh Castle

(17 miles/27.5km)
Bamburgh, NE69 7DF
☎ 01668 214 515
www.bamburghcastle.com
Perched on a basalt outcrop on the very edge of the North Sea at Bamburgh and commanding stunning views of the Farne Islands, Holy Island and the Cheviot hills. The castle houses the Armstrong Museum and the Aviation Artefacts Museum.

Top: Percy Monument Bottom: Statue and Clematis at Alnwick Garden

Events

The International Festival of Music, Song and Dance
www.alnwickfestival.com

The Alnwick Food Festival
www.alnwickfoodfestival.co.uk

Hotels & Dining

Book through local tourist information centre, see Essential Contacts for details.

Something Special

West Acre House

West Acres, NE66 2QA
☎ 01665 510374
www.westacrehouse.co.uk
West Acre House is an imposing elegant detached Edwardian villa situated in its own 1 acre garden, in a beautiful leafy suburb on the outskirts of Alnwick. A quality B&B experience.

White Swan Hotel

16 Bondgate Within, NE66 1TD
☎ 01665 602109
Recently refurbished 300 year old coaching inn. Dine in the Olympic suite, featuring oak panels salvaged from the SS Olympic, sister ship of RMS Titanic. The White Swan is situated in the heart of Alnwick within easy walking distance of Alnwick Castle and Gardens.

The Queens Head Hotel

25 Market Street, NE66 1SS
☎ 01665 604691
Claims to be 'The oldest pub in Alnwick'; this 16th century pub and B&B offers quality accommodation and food. It is located in the centre of Alnwick and is an ideal base from which to explore.

The Sanctuary at The Castle

Alnwick Castle, NE66 1NQ
☎ 01665 511131
email: reservations@thesanctuaryat-thecastle.com

Caffe Tirreno

45 Bondgate Without, NE66 1PR
☎ 01665 605455

Essential Contacts

Tourist Information Centres

Alnwick

The Shambles
☎ 01665 510447

Queen Street
☎ 01665 712313
www.visitalnwick.org.uk

Craster

The Car Park, Craster, NE66 3TW
☎ 01665 576007

Alnwick Playhouse

Bondgate Without, Alnwick, NE66 1PQ
☎ 01665 510785
email: info@alnwickplayhouse.co.uk
www.alnwickplayhouse.co.uk

Landmark Visitors Guide: Northumberland
ISBN: 9781843063810
£7.99

Arundel, West Sussex

Getting There

By Road

Reached by the A27 and is situated between the cities of Chichester and Worthing.

By Rail & Bus

There are train services to Arundel from around the country.

Some coach/bus companies offer a service to Arundel.

You may have to make changes to complete your journey.

Background Briefing

This delightful historic market town has plenty to offer the visitor. The 11th century fairytale castle dominates the skyline. It is the seat of the Duke of Norfolk and is set in forty acres of sweeping grounds and gardens. A magnificent French Gothic-style cathedral faced with Bath stone overlooks the town; it was completed in 1873 to the design of Joseph Hansom, inventor of the Hansom cab.

Stroll along the narrow streets of this picturesque town and discover numerous unusual shops such as The Walking Stick Shop in Tarrant Street, or wander through the nine rooms of Arundel Antiques and Collectables in High Street. Arundel has a variety of pubs, wine bars and restaurants to suit every taste.

Not for the faint-hearted is the Arundel Ghost Experience, which starts from the Town Hall and descends into the dank murky bowels of the Victorian cells underneath.

The Arundel Festival is a week-long extravaganza of Street Theatre, Gallery Trails, Open Air Theatre and much more. The event usually occurs around August Bank Holiday and is an absolute must for all visitors. A Farmers' Market is usually held in The Square on the third Saturday of each month.

Places to Visit

Arundel Castle

Mill Road, BN18 9AB

☎ 01903 882173

www.arundelcastle.org

There are nearly 1,000 years of history at Arundel Castle, situated in magnificent grounds overlooking the River Arun. The home of the Duke of Norfolk the Earl Marshal of England, it is one of the great treasure houses of England, each having its own unique place in history, and is home to priceless works of art.

Arundel Cathedral

Cathedral House, Parsons Hill, BN18 9AY

☎ 01903 882297

The cathedral was founded by Henry 15th Duke of Norfolk, whose old established family own extensive estates around Arundel. The west facade has striking figures of Christ and his apostles and a statue of Mary with her divine child, together with a large rose window adorned with stained glass.

Arundel Museum & Heritage Centre

c/o The Town Hall, Maltravers Street, BN18 9NY

☎ 01903 882268

www.arundelmuseum.org.uk

Exhibit's and photographs giving a glimpse into the development of the town.

Please note, at the time of writing the Museum is undergoing development and may not be located at this address; we recommend you check the website for further information.

Attractions Nearby

Wildfowl & Wetlands Trust

(1 mile/1.5km)

Mill Road, Arundel, BN18 9PB

☎ 01903 883355

www.wwt.org.uk

Arundel Wetland Centre has twenty-six hectares of naturalised landscapes and wetland habitats holding hundreds of exotic wildfowl from around the world. Free safaris on quiet, electric boats are offered everyday weather permitting. Gliding along the waterways of the new Wetlands Discovery area you can discover wild flora and fauna in their natural environment. Walk through the reed beds on a specially designed boardwalk.

Amberley Working Museum

(4 miles/6.5km)

Station Road, Amberley, BN18 9LT

☎ 01798 831370

www.amberleymuseum.co.uk

A thirty-six acre open-air museum dedicated to the industrial heritage of the south-east. The museum is also home to a number of resident craftspeople, who work to traditional methods.

Fontwell Park Racecourse

(6 miles/9.5km)

Fontwell, BN18 0SX

☎ 01243 543335

www.fontwellpark.co.uk

Denmans Gardens

(6 miles/9.5km)

Denmans Lane, Fontwell, BN18 0SU

☎ 01243 542808

www.denmans-garden.co.uk

Situated adjacent to the racecourse. The display of this four acre garden is not only to do with flower colour, but foliage form, texture and, in the autumn, with foliage colour as well.

Arundel Castle

Bignor Roman Villa
(6 miles/9.5km)
Bignor, Pulborough, RH20 1PH
www.bignorromanvilla.co.uk
Impressive remains of a Roman Villa.

Petworth House & Park (NT)
(12 miles/19km)
Petworth, GU28 0AE
☎ 01798 343929
Magnificent country house and park with an internationally important art collection.

Lancing College Chapel
(12 miles/19km)
Lancing College Chapel,
Lancing, BN15 0RW
www.lancingcollege.co.uk
This magnificent Gothic chapel set on the South Downs is the largest school chapel in the world. It was founded in 1868 and dedicated in 1911. An outstanding rose window, the largest in England, was dedicated by the Prince of Wales in 1978.

RSPB Pulborough Brooks
(2 miles/3km)
Pulborough, see web site for how to get there.
www.rspb.org.uk
Set in the heart of beautiful countryside, this reserve is a fantastic day out for people of all ages. Walks lead through hedge-lined paths to viewing areas and hides where volunteers are often on hand to help with wildlife identification.

Events

Farmers' Market
The third Saturday of every month (9am – 1pm).

Hotels & Dining

Book through local Tourist Information Centre, see Essential Contacts for details.

Something Special

The Town House
65 High Street, BN18 9AJ
☎ 01903 883847
www.thetownhouse.co.uk
Stunning architecture and elegant en-suite bedrooms set in a Grade II listed building built around the 1800s.

The Norfolk Arms
High Street, Arundel, BN18 9AJ
☎ 01903 882101
A Georgian coaching inn, set under the battlements of Arundel Castle, with many original features, built over 200 years ago by the tenth Duke of Norfolk.

Swan Hotel Arundel
27–29 High Street, BN18 9AG
☎ 01903 882314
www.fullersinns.co.uk
Elegant Grade II listed building in the centre of town. The hotel has fifteen bedrooms.

Landmark Trust
Foxhall, Charlton. 10 miles/16km from Arundel.
Built 1730, opulent accommodation built by the Duke of Richmond, sleeps 4.

Arundel House Restaurant
11 High Street, BN18 9AD
☎ 01903 882136
www.arundelhouseonline.co.uk

Essential Contacts

Tourist Information Centre
61 High Street, BN18 9AJ
☎ 01903 882268
www.sussexbythesea.com
www.visitsussex.org

Walks
Call at the Tourist Office to pick up self-guided trail leaflets for walks around the town, Arundel Park, the South Downs or along the River Arun.

River Arun Cruises
Mill Road, BN18 9PA
☎ 01903 882609
www.ri011803882609.com
www.riveraruncruises.com
Cruises along the River Arun and motorboat hire.

Arundel Ghost Experience
Duke's Path entrance High Street
Arundel Town Hall
☎ 01903 889821

Ashbourne, Derbyshire

Getting There

By Road

From M6: Junction 15, A50 to Sudbury, A515 to Ashbourne.
From M1: Junction 24, A50 to Sudbury, A515 to Ashbourne.

By Rail & Bus

Nearest railway stations:
Uttoxeter, Derby, Stoke-on-Trent or Buxton.

There are coach/bus services to Ashbourne from around the country although you may have to change to complete your journey.

Background Briefing

Ashbourne nestles below the Peak District limestone plateau and has a milder, more sheltered climate as a result (it is 'an overcoat lighter' goes an old saying). It is a good base for exploring the southern Peak. The limestone dales and villages are renowned for their scenic beauty and well worth exploring. If your visit is in the spring, enquire about the villages holding well dressing exhibitions during your stay.

In town, Church Street is the finest Georgian street in the county after Friargate in Derby. The church is large for such a small 13th century settlement and the tomb-chest of six-year-old Penelope Boothby is exquisite.

Nearby, Dovedale (4 miles), on a sunny summer morning midweek is memorable. The Manifold Valley light railway track is also worth trying from Waterhouses (Cycle Hire) to Hulme End and return (16 miles). Kedleston Hall (NT) with its Robert Adam architecture is well worth visiting as well as the smaller Tissington Hall. If you have not recently been to Chatsworth (home of the Duke and Duchess of Devonshire) it should not be missed. The house and gardens will take up half a day. Nearby is Haddon Hall, claimed to be Britain's most complete non-fortified medieval house. Haddon is close to Bakewell and Chatsworth and the three make for a nice day trip.

Major events in the calendar for Ashbourne include Shrovetide Football (not for the faint of heart); well dressing in Derbyshire villages from May to early summer; Ashbourne Arts Festival at the end of June, featureing local artists and various performances from well known to slightly less well known performers including actors, bands and performance artists. In July, Ashbourne Highland Gathering takes over the town with bagpipes, highland games and the traditional street parade of pipe bands through the town on Sunday morning when the leader of the march attempts to throw his mace over the Green Man inn sign which straddles St Johns Street and is said to be over 25ft high! It is the largest Highland Gathering anywhere outside Scotland.

Ashbourne country show is usually held in August and has a charm of its own with many traditional country show events involving horses, dogs and competitions.

Places to Visit

Although there are not many attractions in Ashbourne, it is however an important hub for visiting the southern Peak District.

Dovedale

Four miles from town. Lovely scenery, SSSI status and footpath from Thorpe Cloud through to Hartington (8 miles/12.5km) and on to the source of the River Dove. Large car park at riverside below the Dovedale stepping stones at Thorpe Cloud, near Ilam.

Carsington Water

(6 miles/10km east of town)
☎ 01629 540478
www.carsingtonwater.com
Large reservoir. Walk around the reservoir (9 miles/14.4km), watersports facilities, bike hire etc.

Walking in the southern Peak

The area is very popular with walkers with many waymarked paths through lovely countryside. Walking books and leaflets available at the Tourist Information centre/local bookshops. For short walks, ask for the books by Pat & Peter Tidsall (Ashbourne Editions).

Attractions Nearby

Chatsworth House

Bakewell DE45 1PP
☎ 01246 565300

Left – Right: Church Street, Ashbourne; Shrovetide football; Sheep farming in the Peak

Top Left – Right: Ashbourne; Churnet Valley; Ashbourne Church
Bottom Left – Right: Tissington Hall; Dovedale; Kedleston Hall

www.chatsworth.org

As well as being one of Britain's most famous and welcoming historic houses Chatsworth has a wide range of attractions for all the family, including the farmyard where you can meet a range of animals, a breathtaking garden and park (including the newly uncovered Quebec garden) and some of the most remarkable water features you're ever likely to see.

Kedleston Hall (NT)

Kedleston, DE22 5JH

☎ 01332 842191

A 18th century masterpiece of neo-classical architecture, designed by Robert Adam. Luxurious state rooms retaining their original collections of paintings and sculpture. The house is set in a magnificent park with a lovely garden at the rear side of the house.

Tissington Hall

Tissington, Ashbourne, DE6 1RA

☎ 01335 350501

www.tissington-hall.com

Built by Francis FitzHerbert in 1609 to replace the moated manor house to the north of the church, it has served as the home for the Fitztterberts for the best part of 400 years.

Hotels & Dining

Book through Tourist Information Centre, see Essential Contacts for details.

Something Special

Turlow Bank

Hognaston, DE6 1PW

☎ 01335 370299

email: turlowbank@w3z.co.uk

www.turlowbank.co.uk

Izaak Walton Hotel

Dovedale, DE6 2AY

☎ 0871 716 2145

Omnia Somnia

The Coach House (B&B),

The Firs, DE6 1HF

☎ 01335 300145

www.omniasomia.co.uk

The Dining Room

33 St John Street, DE6 1GP

☎ 01335 300666

www.thediningroomashbourne.co.uk

Landmark Trust

Alton Railway Station

Sleeps six. Near Alton Towers on site of former railway station, about ten miles from Ashbourne.

Essential Contacts

Tourist Information Centre

Market Place, Ashbourne,
DE6 1EU

☎ 01335 343666

Landmark Visitors Guide:
Peak District
ISBN: 9781843063834; £9.99

Barnard Castle, Durham

Getting There

By Road

M6: J38, A685/A66/A67 (around 35miles/56km). Or A1: Scotch Corner, A66 and right after Gretna Bridge (21miles/33.5km). A1(M): J61, A688 via Bishop Auckland (24miles/38km).

By Rail & Bus

Mainline rail to Bishop Auckland, 15miles/25 km; Darlington, 20miles/30 km.

There are no direct services to Barnard Castle by bus but you may be able to get a local bus from Durham.

Background Briefing

This historic market town with its attractive and varied architecture is developed around the castle and is surrounded by gentle dales and rolling moorland. A walk around the town's cobbled streets will take you past many listed buildings including houses, shops and former

factories. The unusual Octagonal Market Cross, dated 1747, was previously used, at different times, as a Town Hall, courtroom, lock-up and fire station. A blue plaque inside the building reveals the history of this unusual building. Two bullet holes can still be seen in the weather vane on top of the building. They are reputed to have been the result of a shooting match between a volunteer soldier and a local gamekeeper. Barnard Castle, the imposing stronghold of the Balliol family, stands on a high rock overlooking the River Tees. The ruined castle has a splendid great hall and a dominating round-towered keep.

The Bowes Museum in Newgate, offers a fascinating museum experience for all the family. See the greatest collection of European fine and decorative arts in the north of England set in an opulent French-style chateau. The museum has an acclaimed exhibition programme, alongside special events and children's interactive games and activities. One of the great attractions at Bowes Museum is the life-size silver swan, an automaton, which periodically preens itself and appears to catch and swallow a fish. The museum grounds have acres of parkland for pleasant walks, fountains and a parterre garden.

St Mary's Church contains many memorials and relics associated with the Durham Light Infantry as well as interesting stained glass. Take a walk along the river to nearby Egglestone Abbey or pick up a town trail leaflet from the Tourist Information Centre. There are also walking leaflets available for nearby Cotherstone, Romaldkirk and the rest of Teesdale. A weekly market is still held on Wednesdays and a Farmers' Market on the first Saturday of every month. The

town has a variety of unusual shops including craft and antique shops. The lovely town of Richmond is 15 miles/24km to the southwest, via the A66.

Places to Visit

Barnard Castle (EH)

DL12 9AT

☎ 01833 638212

Set on a high rock above the River Tees. Taking its name from Bernard de Balliol, who rebuilt it in the 12th century, it includes a fine great hall and round-towered keep. Unsuccessfully besieged by the Scots in 1216, it was confiscated when John de Balliol, briefly King of Scotland, was deposed by Edward I. The castle was partly dismantled in 1630 to furnish materials for Sir Henry Vane's new Raby Castle.

The Bowes Museum

Barnard Castle, DL12 8NP

☎ 01833 690606

www.thebowesmuseum.org.uk

The Bowes Museum offers a fascinating museum experience for all the family. Enjoy the greatest collection of European fine and decorative arts in the north of England and an acclaimed exhibition programme, alongside special events and children's activities.

Attractions Nearby

Egglestone Abbey

1 mile south of Barnard Castle, on a minor road off B6277.

The charming ruins of a small monastery of Premonstratensian 'white canons' picturesquely set above a bend in the River Tees near Barnard Castle. Remains include much of the 13th century church and a range of living quarters.

Eggleston Hall Gardens

(7 miles/11km)

Eggleston, DL12 0AG

☎ 01833 650115

www.egglestonhall.co.uk
'The Secret Garden of the North', try the delightful garden walk with surprises round every corner.

Rokeby Park

(3 miles/5km)
Barnard Castle, DL12 9RZ
☎ 01609 748612
email: enquiries@rokebypark.com
www.rokebypark.com
18th century Palladian-style country house with paintings and period furniture on display, together with a unique collection of needlework pictures by Anne Morritt and an unusual 'Print Room'.

Thorpe Farm Centre

Thorpe Farm, Greta Bridge, Barnard Castle, DL12 9TY
☎ 01833 627242
email: info@thorpefarm.co.uk
www.thorpefarm.co.uk
Offers an array of attractions for the whole family.

Raby Castle

(6 miles/9.5km)
Staindrop, DL2 3AH
☎ 01833 660202
www.rabycastle.com
The castle has well-preserved halls and chambers and the grandest medieval kitchen in England. Outside are walled gardens, a 200 acre deer park and a coach and carriage museum.

Hotels & Dining

Book through Barnard Castle Tourist Information Centre, see Essential Contcts for details.

Hotels & Dining
Something Special

Landmark Trust

The Grammar School, Kirby Hill 10 miles/16km southwest of Barnard Castle. Sleeps four.

Morritt Arms Hotel

Greta Bridge, DL12 9SE
☎ 01833 627232
www.themorritt.co.uk
This beautiful hotel provides country accommodation for holiday makers as well as those wanting to get away for weekend breaks. Diners are always welcome to eat in the contemporary restaurant, bistro, bar or one of the many lounges.

Marwood House

98 Calgate, DL12 8BJ
☎ 01833 637493
email: marwoodhouse@yahoo.co.uk
www.marwoodhouse.co.uk
Tastefully furnished hotel replete with tapestries and embroideries in a Grade II Victorian building.

Red Well Inn

Harmire Road DL12 8QJ
www.redwellinn.info
Country inn on the outskirts of the town. Comfortable accommodation and good food.

Blagraves House

30–32 The Bank, DL12 8PN
☎ 01833 637668
www.blagraves.com
16th century Blagraves House reputed to have housed Oliver Cromwell in 1648.

Bailie's

7 The Bank, DL12 8PH
☎ 01833 630700
Renowned for good food.

Sport

Barnard Castle Golf Club

Harmire Road, DL12 8QN
☎ 01833 638 355
email: sec@barnardcastlegolfclub.org.uk
www.barnardcastlegolfclub.org.uk

Essential Contacts

Tourist Information Centre

'Woodleigh', Flatts Road, Barnard Castle, DL12 8AA
☎ 01833 690909
email: tourism@teesdale.gov.uk
www.visitteesdale.co.uk

Top – Bottom: The Crescent; Relaxing afternoon in Bath; Christmas Market at dusk; Roman Baths

Getting There

By Road

M4 exit J18, south on A46.

By Rail & Bus

Mainline companies operate a service into Bath Spa railway station.

Main bus companies operate a service into Bath Bus Station although you may have to make changes to complete your journey.

Background Briefing

The Unesco World Heritage Site of Bath with its combination of wonderful Georgian architecture, Roman sites and a plethora of museums is one of England's most beautiful places to visit. This compact city is easily explored on foot and a pleasant walk will take the visitor to the major attractions. The Pump Room is at the heart of the city where spa water still flows from the fountain overlooking the natural hot spring. The nearby Roman Baths are the best-preserved religious spa from the ancient world.

The Abbey with its fan vaulting and brilliant stained glass is not to be missed, as is the Guildhall with its splendid Georgian interior. The 18th century Assembly Rooms house the Museum of Fashion, which has a collection of contemporary and historical dress. Queen's Square, the Circus and the Royal Crescent are fine examples of Georgian elegance. No 1, Royal Crescent, a magnificently restored and authentically furnished town house, is now open to the public.

Top quality entertainment is provided at the Theatre Royal which has three auditoria, the Main House, the Ustinov and the Egg Theatre for children and young people. The Pulteney Bridge, designed by Robert Adam, is one of the world's most beautiful bridges. Steps from the bridge lead down to the river where cruises depart and riverside walks can be taken. There is so much to see in this vibrant, thriving city, which has superb shopping and award-winning restaurants.

Self-guided walking trails are available at the Tourist Information Centre in the Abbey Churchyard; several guided walking tours are available as well as open-top bus tours. Jane Austen knew Bath as a fashionable spa resort and today visitors can bathe in the natural mineral-rich waters or enjoy a range of treatments at the Thermae Bath Spa. On the outskirts of the town, the Bath Skyline walk is six miles of way marked trails, passing through hidden valleys, tranquil woodlands and a patchwork of meadows rich in wildlife.

Places to Visit

Bath Abbey

12 Kingston Buildings, BA1 1LT

☎ 01225 422462

www.bathabbey.org

The Abbey stands at the heart of the city of Bath; during the past twelve and a half centuries three different churches have occupied the site.

Roman Baths

Abbey Church Yard, BA1 1LZ

☎ 01225 477785

www.romanbaths.co.uk

The best preserved spa from the ancient world.

Thermae Bath Spa

The Hetling Pump Room, Hot Bath Street, BA1 1SJ

☎ 0844 888 0844

email: reservations@thermaebathspa.com

www.thermaebathspa.com

The Building of Bath Museum

Discover how Georgian Bath was developed.

Find out more about these attractions by visiting: www.bath-preservation-trust.org.uk

Fashion Museum

Assembly Rooms, Bennett Street, BA1 2QH

☎ 01225 477173

www.fashionmuseum.co.uk

A world-class collection of contemporary and historical dresses.

The Jane Austen Centre

40 Gay Street, Queen Square, BA1 2NT

☎ 01225 443000

www.janeausten.co.uk

See a fascinating snapshot of life during Regency times.

The American Museum in Britain

(3 miles/5km)

Claverton Manor BA2 7BD

☎ 01225 460503

Furnished rooms trace the American way of life from colonial times to the mid-19th century. Display of American quilts. Interactive activities for children. Forty acres of grounds open to the public including a replica of George Washington's flower garden.

Parade Gardens

Grand Parade, BA2 4DF
Delightful gardens overlooking the River Avon and Pulteney Bridge.

Prior Park Landscape Garden

Ralph Allen Drive, BA2 5AH
Beautiful and intimate 18th century landscape garden.

Royal Victoria Park

Marlborough Lane, BA1 2NQ
Covering fifty-seven acres the park has something for everyone.

Sydney Gardens

Sydney Road, BA2 6NT
Bath's oldest park and often visited by Jane Austen who lived at number 4 Sydney Place.

The Theatre Royal

Sawclose, BA1 1ET
☎ 01225 448844
www.theatreroyal.org.uk
Brimming with history, the Theatre Royal Bath is one of the oldest and most beautiful theatres in Britain.

Hotels & Dining

Book through local Tourist Information Centre, see Essential Contacts for details.

Something Special

Macdonald Bath Spa Hotel

Sydney Road, BA2 6JF
☎ 0870 4008222
www.bathspa-hotel.co.uk
Butler-led service, private suites, fine dining, and state of the art spa with thermal suite including rock sauna, ice room, infrared room, hydro pool, six treatment rooms, indoor pool, gym.

Dukes

Great Pulteney Street, BA2 4DN
☎ 01225 787960
www.dukesbath.co.uk
A magnificent Grade I Palladian style Town House Hotel.

The Hole in the Wall

16–17 George Street, BA1 2EH
☎ 01225 425242
www.theholenthewall.co.uk
Modern British cuisine in the oldest restaurant in Bath.

The Bathwick Boatman

Forester Road, Bathwick, BA2 6QP
☎ 01225 428844
www.bathwickboatman.com
Unique and pretty riverside restaurant (circa 1833), 5–10 minutes stroll from the city centre and overlooking the Avon.

Guided Walking Tours

The Mayor's Guides Free Walking Tours

The Mayors Office, Guildhall
☎ 01225 477411
A general historical and architectural introduction to the city.

Jane Austen Walking Tours

☎ 01225 443000
Find the places where Jane lived, walked, visited and shopped, and discover Bath's fascinating history.

Ghost Walks

98 Lower Oldfield Park, BA2 3HS
☎ 01225 350512
Walk through the ancient streets of the Roman city of Bath.

Bus Tours

Bath Bus Company

6 North Parade, BA1 1LF
☎ 01225 3304449
www.bathbuscompany.com

Top: Pulteney Bridge
Bottom: Pump Room

Boat Tours

Bath City Boat Trips

York Street BA1 1NG
☎ 07974 560197
www.bathcityboattrips.com
Also other pleasure cruises start from Pulteney Bridge.

Essential Contacts

Tourist Information Centre

Abbey Chambers, Abbey Church Yard, Bath, BA1 1LY
☎ 0906 711 2000

Bath International Music Festival 2008

www.efestivals.co.uk/festivals/bath/2008
www.visitbath.co.uk

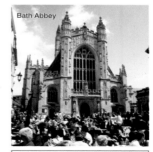

Bath Abbey

Landmark Publishing is grateful to Bath Tourism Plus for providing the images on page 19.
www.visitbath.co.uk

Berwick-upon-Tweed, Northumberland

Getting There

By Road

Situated just off the A1 next to the Scottish Border.

By Rail & Bus

Berwick-upon-Tweed is situated on the East Coast Main Line.

There are coach/bus services to Berwick-upon-Tweed from around the country although you may have to make changes to complete the journey.

Background Briefing

Berwick-upon-Tweed is a fascinating old market town, built mainly of stone with a variety of good pubs and restaurants. Its position on the border with Scotland led to the town changing hands no fewer than fourteen times in the two centuries up to 1482. Interestingly, its football team plays in the Scottish League. Take a walk around the most complete set of Tudor walls in Europe, built to protect the town from Scottish raids, and admire Georgian

Top – Bottom: Berwick Ramparts; A house just outisde the protection of the ramparts; Bass Rock and horses

buildings, the colony of mute swans and views south to the Holy Island of Lindisfarne.

There are excellent views of the three bridges over the Tweed from the ramparts; the 17th century stone bridge has fifteen arches while the spectacular Victorian railway viaduct has twenty-eight arches and soars thirty-eight metres above the river. Pleasant walks can be taken along the river passing the three bridges in close succession. Berwick Barracks is well worth a visit as it houses three museums including the museum of the King's Own Scottish Borderers. Opposite the barracks is the Holy Trinity and St Mary Church (see below).

The spired town hall in Marygate contains the original gaol complete with condemned cell, branding irons, shackles and leg irons. Built in a converted maltings is the Maltings Theatre and Arts Centre with a year-round programme of the best in theatre, film, music, comedy and dance. Complete with a restaurant and bar, it is the premiere arts centre for north Northumberland and the Borders. If you're in town on a Wednesday or Saturday there's a street market to explore. The beautiful Northumbrian countryside and the nearby Heritage Coast ensure that visiting Berwick is a rewarding experience.

Places to Visit

The Barracks

The Parade, TD15 1BN
☎ 01289 304493
The oldest purpose built military barracks in Britain, which now houses three museums. Berwick Barracks is an EH site. The admission charge provides access to the Regimental Museum, the exhibition 'By Beat of Drum', Berwick Borough Museum and Art Gallery, and the Gymnasium Gallery of

contemporary art.

Holy Trinity and St Mary Church

The Parade, TD15 1ED
☎ 01289 306136
A unique Cromwellian church that has 16th century Flemish glass and Lutyens reredos. The most northerly church of the Church of England. Noted for its Presbyterian style of architecture.

Maltings Theatre & Arts Centre

Eastern Lane, TD15 1AJ
☎ 01289 330999
For a selection of drama, music, dance and film visit the website to see what's on.
www.maltingsberwick.co.uk

The Swan Centre for Leisure

Tweedmouth TD15 2AS
☎ 01289 330603
Leisure pool with flume and wave machine plus full range of sports, leisure facilities and children's holiday programme.

Wine and Spirit Museum & Victorian Chemist Shop

Place Green TD15 9YF
☎ 01289 305153

Cell Block Museum & Town Hall

Marygate
☎ 01289 330900
Bygone days, captured through historical artefacts.

Attractions Nearby

Chain Bridge Honey Farm

(5 miles/8km)
Horncliffe, Berwick-upon-Tweed, TD15 2XT
☎ 01289 386362
www.chainbridgehoney.co.uk
Discover more about bees and buy natural honey and beeswax products.

Paxton House & Country Park

(5 miles/8km)
Berwick-upon-Tweed, TD15 1SZ
☎ 01289 386291
www.paxtonhouse.co.uk
Set in eighty acres on the banks of the River Tweed, Paxton House is a hidden gem. Built by the Adam brothers in 1758, it is one of the finest examples of an 18th century Palladian country house in Britain.

Holy Island

(15 miles/24km)
TD15 2SH
☎ 01289 389244
Head south out of Berwick on the A1. The island is approached across a causeway at low tide. Check the times of the tide before you set off; once the tide comes in you are on the island until the next low tide! Visit Lindisfarne Priory, one of the most important centres of early Christianity in Anglo-Saxon England. A museum tells the fascinating story of the monks who lived there. Dominating the island is Lindisfarne Castle, a Romantic 16th century castle with spectacular views, transformed by Lutyens into an Edwardian holiday home.

Events

Greenses Gala

This annual event takes place in August in the Greenses area of Berwick. With continuous music, games, produce stalls, entertainment and children's competitions; a real family fun day.

Slow Food

For details of the food festival and suppliers of local produce visit www.slowfoodberwick.org.uk

Hotels & Dining

Try the local Tourist Information Centre, see Essential Contacts for details.

Berwick-upon-Tweed

Something Special

No 1 Sallyport

Berwick-upon-Tweed, TD15 1EZ
☎ 01289 308827
email: info@sallyport.co.uk
www.sallyport.co.uk
No 1 Sallyport is a boutique hotel located within the town centre of Berwick offering five-star gold award-winning accommodation, consisting of six luxurious, exciting, individually designed rooms.

Queens Head Hotel

6 Sandgate, Berwick-upon-Tweed, TD15 1EP
☎ 01289 307852
www.queensheadberwick.co.uk
Charming town centre hotel, adjacent to Tudor walls.

Kings Arms Hotel

43 Hide Hill, TD15 1EJ
Featuring a blend of 18th century architecture and modern facilities. Has a lovely walled garden to the rear of the hotel.

Marshall Meadows Country House Hotel

Berwick-upon-Tweed, TD15 1UT
☎ 01289 331133
email: gm.marshallmeadows@classiclodges.co.uk
www.classiclodges.co.uk

A Georgian mansion, this is England's most northerly hotel with its own woodland gardens just 400 metres from the border.

Cobbled Yard Hotel & Restaurant

40 Walkergate, TD15 1DJ
☎ 01289 308407

Berlino Restaurant

37 West Street TD15 2LB
☎ 01289 306149

The Lowry Trail

You can explore the town walls and bridges by following the Lowry Trail, which follows in the footsteps of L.S. Lowry as he wandered the town on holiday, painting many familiar views. The interpretation panels are scattered around Berwick, drawing the follower over the river into Tweedmouth and Spittal.

Essential Contacts

Tourist Information Centre

106 Marygate, TD15 1BN
☎ 01289 330733
email: tourism@berwick-upon-tweed.gov.uk
www.berwick-upon-tweed.gov.uk

Landmark Visitors Guide: Northumberland
ISBN: 9781843063810
£7.99

Enjoy a day at the races

Getting There

By Road

Over the Humber Bridge from the M180 or M62, A63 and join the A164.

By Rail & Bus

There are trains calling at Beverley Railway Station from around the country although you may have to change to complete your journey.

There are coach/bus operators offering a service to Beverley from around the country.

Background Briefing

Beverley, in the East Riding of Yorkshire, is an historic and beautiful market town famous for its 13th century Minster, its market and its music. Wander around cobbled lanes with intriguing names reflecting life in former times and discover antique and craft shops, historic pubs and fine Georgian and Victorian terraces. The Saturday Market Place still hosts a lively market and also serves as a venue for Food and Christmas Festivals and classic car displays. The Guildhall in Register Square, although substantially remodelled, still has some 15th century timbers. The courtroom has a stucco ceiling created by the Swiss-Italian stuccoist Giuseppe

Cortese in 1762 and an imposing facade modelled on a Greek temple was added around 1830. Beverley Minster with its soaring twin towers is a magnificent example of medieval Gothic architecture and contains the Percy tomb, a masterpiece of medieval art. A climb to the top of the bell tower is rewarded with spectacular views of the town and surrounding countryside. Nearby is the restored Dominican Friary, now used as a Youth Hostel, with medieval paintings and murals. St Mary's Church has a fine 14th century West Front and a decorated ceiling depicting Kings of England. A stroll along Beverley Beck to Crane Hill Wharf will find the 'Syntan', a former working barge, which has been lovingly restored by the Beverley Barge Preservation Society. Walk to Westwood, an attractive windswept common, for country walks, kite flying and picnics in open pastureland. Historic Westwood is also home to Beverley racecourse, now a major player in the horseracing calendar. Beverley is famous for its annual festivals of early music, chamber music and folk music, maintaining its ancient tradition as a centre of musical excellence.

Away from the town are the villages and countryside of the York-

shire Wolds, Hull with its rich maritime history and historic old town, the Humber Bridge Country Park with superb views and bird watching opportunities and Bridlington offering traditional seaside fare.

Places to Visit

Beverley Minster
Minster Yard North, HU17 0DP
www.beverleyminster.org.uk
One of Britain's finest examples of medieval architecture featuring 16th century misericords, a Saxon sanctuary chair, and the magnificent Percy tomb.

Beverley Art Gallery
Champney Road, HU17 8HE
☎ 01482 392780
The Gallery holds the largest collection of works by celebrated local

artist, Frederick Elwell.

Barge Preservation Society
Cranes Hill Wharf, Beckside HU17
OGG
☎ 01482 872803

St Mary's Church
North Bar

The Racecourse
York Road HU17 8QZ
☎ 01482 867488/882645
www.beverley-racecourse.co.uk

Attractions Nearby

The Deep
Hull, HU1 4DP
☎ 01482 381000
www.thedeep.co.uk
This is one of the most spectacular
aquariums in the world and an
award-winning family attraction,
home to forty sharks and over
3,500 fish.

Arctic Corsair
36 High Street, Hull, HU1 1NQ
☎ 01482 658838
This beautiful old ship was built in
Beverley in 1965 and was one of
the last 'side winder' fishing boats
to operate out of Hull. A veteran
ship from the 'Cod Wars', the boat
had an interesting and exciting life
on the seas which came to an end in
1987. The vessel is now open to the
public, a museum to the seafaring
past of the city.

Burnby Hall Gardens
(18 miles/29km)
Pocklington, YO42 2QF
www.burnbyhallgardens.com
Delightful gardens with a national
collection of water lilies in two lakes
set in beautiful gardens.

Burton Constable Hall
(14.5 miles/23.5km)
Skirlaugh, HU11 4LN
www.burtonconstable.com
☎ 01964 562400
A large Elizabethan mansion set in

a 300 acre park with nearly thirty
rooms open to the public.

**Humber Bridge Country
Park**
(9 miles/14.5km)
Ferriby Road, Hessle, Hull
☎ 01482 395207
The reserve at the country park is a
hive of wildlife and you can explore
various trails including the Phoenix
Sculpture Trail.

Skidby Windmill
(4.5 miles/7km)
Skidby, Cottingham HU16 5TF
☎ 01482 848405
Yorkshire's last working windmill
whose adjacent warehouses form
the Museum of East Riding Rural
Life.

Wilberforce House
23–25 High Street, Hull
HU1 1NE
☎ 01482 613902
www.wilberforce2007.com
This 17th century Merchant's
House was the birthplace of William
Wilberforce and now, after a mul-
timillion pound refurbishment, is a
museum telling the story of slavery
and its abolition.

Events

**Beverley and East Riding
Early Music Festival**

**Beverley Chamber Music
Festival**

Christmas Festival

Folk Festival

Kite flying Festival

Hotels & Dining
Try the Tourist Information Centre,
see Essential Contacts for details.

Something Special

The Lairgate in Beverley
30–32 Lairgate, HU17 8EP
☎ 01482 882141

Top: Cows on Westwood Black Mill
Bottom: Beverley town centre

www.thelairgateinbeverley.co.uk
Conveniently situated in the centre
of Beverley in a listed Georgian
building.

**Tickton Grange Hotel &
Restaurant**
Tickton, HU17 9SH
☎ 01964 543666
www.ticktongrange.co.uk
A Georgian country house hotel
just three miles from Beverley
with award-winning cuisine in the
Champagne restaurant.

Beverley Arms Hotel
North Bar Within, HU17 8DD
☎ 01482 869241
The menu at the restaurant here
is varied with traditional, freshly
prepared food.

Cerutti 2
Station Square, HU17 0AS
☎ 01482 866700
Enjoy modern European food and
seafood in the rejuvenated old
waiting room at Beverley Station.

Essential Contacts

**Beverley Tourist
Information Centre**
34 Butcher Row, HU17 0AB
☎ 01482 391672

**Hull Tourist Information
Centre**
1 Paragon Street, Hull, HU1 3NA
☎ 01482 223559
www.realyorkshire.co.uk

Top – **Bottom**: Boston Stump; Cyclists in front of Boston Stump; Boston Marina; Town centre; Boston Guildhall

Getting There

By Road

Via the A16, A17, A52 and the A1/M1.

By Rail & Bus

Main East Coast line to Grantham, connection to Boston.

Various operators have a bus service to Boston, check online for more details.

Background Briefing

This bustling and attractive market town was once an important port for the Hanseatic traders of northern Europe. It has a working dock and indeed for a part of the 13th century was the leading port in England. A walk through Boston's intriguing streets takes the visitor past many fine buildings from diverse periods. The Guildhall, recently restored by a lottery grant, dates from the 14th century and has been used as a courtroom, museum and gaol. It was used during the trial and imprisonment of the Pilgrim Fathers in September 1607.

The Custom House was built in 1725 and Fydell House in 1746; the latter is unquestionably the grandest house in town. Shodfriars Hall in South Street is perhaps the most substantial timber-framed building in Boston. Originally a Dominican Friary dating from the 13th century, Blackfriars Arts Centre presents a variety of live shows, events and international films. Fine produce is offered for sale in Boston open-air market on Wednesdays and Saturdays. Boston has an eclectic range of shops and restaurants, fascinating architecture and is surrounded by pleasant countryside. There is a monthly Farmers' Market every third Wednesday.

Places to Visit

St Botolph's Church
Market Place
☎ 01205 362992
www.parish-of-boston.org.uk
Largest parish church in England; the tower is 272ft high, known locally as Boston Stump.

St Mary's Guildhall
South Street, PE21 6HT
www.lincolnshire.gov.uk
Recently renovated and due to reopen in 2008. A museum telling the history of the medieval Guild of St Mary and the story of this amazing building, used as Boston's court, gaol and town hall.

Blackfriars Arts Centre
Spain Lane, PE21 6HP
☎ 01205 363108
www.blackfriars.uk.com
Visit the website for details of what's on.

The Maud Foster Mill
Willoughby Road, PE21 9EG
☎ 01205 352188
www.maudfoster.co.uk
Britain's tallest working windmill, sells organic flour and porridge oats.

Maritime Leisure Cruises
Boston Marina, PE21 9JU
www.maritimecruises.co.uk
River and sea trips departing from Boston. See website for details.

Attractions Nearby

Sibsey Trader Windmill (EH)
Sibsey, PE22 0SY
☎ 01205 750036
Working windmill originally built in 1877, awith ward winning tearoom. Organic flour for sale.

RSPB – Freiston Shore Nature Reserve
(5 miles/8km)
Freiston Shore, PE22 0LY
☎ 01205 724678

www.rspb.org.uk
From Boston, take the A52 road towards Skegness. Upon reaching Haltoft End after two miles, turn right and follow the brown tourism signs from here directing you to RSPB Freiston Shore reserve.

RSPB – Frampton Marsh
(6.5miles/10.5km)
Frampton
☎ 01205 724678
www.rspb.org.uk
Reached from Frampton village, south of Boston. Turn off the A16 at Kirton, signposted to Frampton, pass through Frampton village and follow the signposts from there to RSPB Frampton Marsh nature reserve. The road terminates at the reserve car park after about 2.8 miles (4.5km).

Tattershall Castle (NT)
(16 miles/26km)
Tattershall, LN4 4LR
☎ 01526 342543
Explore this medieval castle rising dramatically above the Lincolnshire countryside. Children can dress up and play with Tudor toys and medieval costumes. Nearby is the Battle of Britain Memorial Flight.

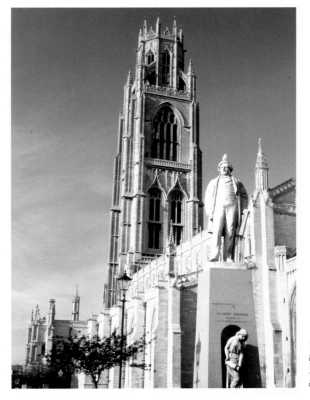
Boston Stump

Events

Boston Party in the Park
The highlight of the cultural calendar is held in July. Check on the internet for more details. The Party is Lincolnshire's largest free weekend-long music festival and features bands and musicians from all over the county.

Spalding Flower Parade & Festival Weekend
www.flowerparade.org
Held in early May; see website for more details of times and dates.

Hotels & Dining
Book through local Tourist Information Centre, see Essential Contacts for details.

Something Special

The White Hart
1–5 High Street, Boston, PE 21 8SH
☎ 01205 311900
www.whitehartboston.com
This impressive Georgian-style town centre hotel on the banks of the River Witham offers a range of comfortable facilities, with twenty-three bedrooms, including a family room and a room with a four-poster bed, ideal for honeymoons and special occasions.

The New England Hotel
49 Wide Bargate, Boston, PE 21 6SH
☎ 01205 365255
Situated in the centre of Boston the hotel is ideal for exploring historic Boston and the surrounding fens, wetlands and coastlines.

Bizzarro
23 Wormgate, PE21 6NR
☎ 0845 0175 644
www.bizzarro.biz
Traditional Italian food in comfortable, cosy surroundings.

Restaurant 45
45 West Street, PE21 8QN
☎ 0845 0175 626
Specialises in modern English cuisine with Italian influence.

Landmark Publishing gratefully acknowledges Lincolnshire Tourism Ltd for the use of the images on these pages. www.visitlincolnshire.com

Top – Bottom: Balloons over Bristol; Bristol Cathedral; Pero's Bridge; SS Great Britain; St Nicholas Markets; Clifton Suspension Bridge; Children at the Bristol City Museum & Art Gallery

Getting There

By Road

From M4 exit at J19, M32 into city centre.
From M5 exit at J18, A4 Portway into city centre.

By Rail & Bus

Mainline trains run into Bristol Temple Meads from stations between London Paddington, Cardiff, Edinburgh and Penzance.

The main coach/bus companies provide a service to Bristol Bus Station from around the country.

Background Briefing

Bustling Bristol, formerly the second largest port in the country, still has docks and a lively harbour area. The sturdy ships once built here gave rise to the expression 'all shipshape and Bristol fashion'. There is so much to see down by the harbour where restaurants, bars, museums, arts centres and Isambard Kingdom Brunel's maritime masterpiece, the SS Great Britain, compete for your attention. Visit the endlessly fascinating 'Explore-at-Bristol', an interactive science centre complete with planetarium, stroll along the quayside past former warehouses and tea sheds, or take a trip on a ferry. One of the best ways to explore Bristol is on foot, although it is a little hilly, and wander through streets lined with medieval, Georgian and Victorian architecture.

Don't miss the magnificent Queen's Square with its elegant restored Regency houses and picturesque park, or King Street lined with period architecture and historic inns. The Cabot Tower, built in 1897 to commemorate John Cabot's voyage to America in 1497, is a well-known landmark. Climb the spiral staircase to the top of the tower for stunning views over the city. Bristol Cathedral is the major example of a 'Hall Church' in Great Britain and one of the finest anywhere in the world. The beautiful Eastern Lady Chapel, with its vivid colours and 14th century glass, and the Norman Chapter House should not be missed. St Mary Redcliffe with fine Gothic architecture and elegant spire is also worthy of a visit and is one of the most beautiful churches in England.

In the evening dine out at a gourmet restaurant or visit one of the theatres. Bristol is a shopper's paradise with independent shops, boutiques and high street names. A Farmers' Market is held every Wednesday and an Arts and Craft Market at weekends. On the first Sunday of each month there is a Slow Food Market in Corn Street. As if this was not enough there is also stunning Georgian architecture in Clifton as well as Brunel's world-famous Clifton Suspension Bridge.

Places to Visit

Brunel's SS Great Britain & Maritime Heritage Centre

Great Western Dockyard, Gas Ferry Road, BS1 6TY
☎ 0117 926 0680
www.ssgreatbritain.org
The world's first ocean-going, propeller driven iron ship. Experience life on board in Victorian times and visit the three-storey-tall moving engine.

Bristol International Balloon Festival

Left: Neptune Statue; Middle Top: The locks at the entrance to Bristol Harbour; Middle Bottom: Victoria Rooms; Right: The mirrored orangarium

British Empire & Commonwealth Museum

Clock Tower Yard, Temple Meads, BS1 6QH

☎ 0117 925 4980

www.empiremuseum.co.uk

Housed inside Brunel's 19th century railway station, this award-winning museum tells the story of Britain's overseas empire. Interactive exhibits, computer games and puzzles are part of this amazing experience. Discover the history of the greatest empire the world has ever known.

Explore-At-Bristol

Anchor Road, Harbourside, BS1 5DB

☎ 0845 345 1235

www.at-bristol.org.uk

Science is brought alive at this exciting venue using the very latest multi-media techniques. You can find out how your brain and body tick, investigate optical illusions, play with light and mirrors and watch live and interactive shows.

Other Places to Visit

Arnolfini

16 Narrow Quay, BS1 4QA

☎ 0117 917 2300/01

www.arnolfini.org.uk

Arnolfini is one of Europe's leading centres for the contemporary arts in a wonderful waterside location.

Bristol Cathedral

College Green, BS1 5TJ

☎ 0117 926 4879

www.bristol-cathedral.co.uk

Founded in 1140 as a monastery, of which the Chapter House and Abbey Gatehouse remain, together with other remains within Bristol Cathedral School. The eastern end of the Cathedral, especially in the Choir, gives Bristol Cathedral a unique place in the development of British and European architecture. The nave, choir and aisles are all the same height, making a large hall: it is a major example of a 'Hall Church' in Great Britain and one of the finest anywhere in the world.

In 1539 the Abbey was closed and the partially rebuilt nave was demolished. The building became the Cathedral Church in 1542. In 1868 plans were drawn up to rebuild the nave to its medieval design. The architect, G.E. Street, found the original pillar bases, so the dimensions are much the same as those of the abbey church.

Bristol's City Museum & Art Gallery

Queen's Road, BS8 1RL

☎ 0117 922 3571

www.bristol.gov.uk/museums

The region's largest museum and art gallery with an outstanding and diverse range of objects.

Bristol Industrial Museum

Princes Wharf, Wapping Road, BS1 4RN

☎ 0117 925 1470

www.bristol-city.gov.uk

All the wonder of Bristol's industrial heritage housed in an historic transit shed with larger exhibits outside. The museum also tells the story of the port of Bristol and its involvement in the slave trade.

Bristol Zoo Gardens

Clifton, BS8 3HA

☎ 0117 974 7399

www.bristolzoo.org.uk

Bristol Zoo Gardens is based in a twelve acre site in Clifton.

Cabot Tower

Brandon Hill, Great George Street, BS1 5QD

☎ 0117 9260767

A Bristol landmark some thirty-two metres high. Climb to the top on a clear day and take some amazing pictures of Bristol.

Georgian House Museum

7 Great George Street, BS1 5RR

☎ 0117 921 1362
www.bristol.gov.uk
This 18th century townhouse, the former home of a Bristol sugar merchant, has been restored to its original glory.

Red Lodge Museum

Park Row, BS1 5LJ
☎ 0117 921 1360
www.bristol.gov.uk
A 16th century house, furnished in both Elizabethan and Georgian styles, and a beautiful Tudor-style knot garden filled with flowers and shrubs.

Attractions Nearby

Blaise Castle House Museum and Estate

(4.5 miles/7km)
Henbury Road, Henbury
BS10 7QS
☎ 0117 903 9818
visitbristol.co.uk
A 19th century mansion set in 400 acres of parkland and home to a social history collection. Discover Victorian toilets and baths, kitchen and laundry equipment, model trains, dolls, toys and period costume.

Tyntesfield (NT)

(7.5 miles/12km)
Wraxall, BS48 1NT
☎ 0844 800 4966
A spectacular Gothic Revival country house and estate with a working kitchen garden. Definitely worth visiting but timed ticket only available on arrival.

Events

Bristol has several festivals throughout the year. Enquire at the Tourist Information Centre for further details.

Bristol Harbour Festival

Ashton Court Festival

International Balloon Fiesta

International Kite Festival

Christmas Market

Encounters Festival

Hotels & Dining

Book through local Tourist Information Centre, see Essential Contacts for details.

Something Special

Mercure Holland House Hotel & Spa

Redcliffe Hill, BS1 6SQ
☎ 0117/9689900
www.mercure-uk.com
A luxury four-star city centre hotel with fitness suite and spa, just ten minutes walk from Bristol Temple Meads train station.

Bristol Marriott Royal Hotel

College Green, BS1 5TA
☎ 0117 9255100
www.marriott.com
Wonderful location next to the cathedral and the historic waterfront with Romanesque indoor swimming pool, sauna, whirlpool and fitness centre.

Arbi 'n' Tap Floating Cafe Restaurant

The Corrine, Marin Narrow Quay, BS1 4QA
☎ 0117 954 4844
www.arbintap.co.uk
The Arbi 'n' Tap is a beautiful restaurant housed in a newly built replica Severn trow moored in an historic dock. The restaurant is candlelit at night creating a unique dining experience.

Fishers Restaurant

35 Princess Victoria Street, Clifton Village, BS8 4BX
☎ 0117 974 7044
A seafood restaurant in the heart of Clifton Village, just around the corner from Avon Gorge and the Clifton Suspension Bridge. There is something for everyone here from grilled Canadian lobsters to beer-battered haddock and chips.

Essential Contacts

Useful website:
www.visitbristol.co.uk

Bristol Tourist Information Centre

Explore-At-Bristol, Anchor Road, Harbourside, Bristol, BS1 5DB
☎ 0906 711 2191

Guided Walks

Available at weekends; try the Bristol Highlights walk or the Pirates walk.

Bristol Hippodrome

St. Augustine's Parade, BS1 4UZ
www.bristolhippodrome.org.uk

Bristol Old Vic

King Street, Bristol, BS1 4ED
☎ 0117 987 7877
www.bristol-old-vic.co.uk

City Sightseeing – The Bristol Tour

Departs from city centre
Central Bristol, BS1 4AH
☎ 0870 444 0654
www.bristolvisitor.co.uk

Bristol Ferry Boat Company

MB Tempora Welsh Back, BS1 4SP
☎ 0117 9273416
www.bristolferry.com

The Bristol Packet Boat Trips

Wapping Wharf, Gas Ferry Road, BS1 6UN
☎ 0117 926 8157
www.bristolpacket.co.uk

Landmark Publishing gratefully acknowledges Destination Bristol for the images supplied on page 26.
www.visitbristol.co.uk

Landmark Visitors Guide: Somerset (Includes Bristol); ISBN: 9781843063285; £9.99

Bury St Edmunds, Suffolk

Top: Abbey Gardens; Bottom: Bury Cathedral

Getting There

By Road

Situated just off the A14.

By Rail & Bus

Bury St Edmunds has its own railway station, connecting to Cambridge, Ipswich and the London–Norwich line.

There are coach/bus connections into Bury St Edmunds from around the country although you may have to make changes to complete your journey.

Background Briefing

Bury St Edmunds is an historic market town serving a large rural area. The biggest street markets in East Anglia are still held here on Wednesdays and Saturdays. The town evolved around a Benedictine Monastery, founded in 1020. The ruins can still be seen in the beautiful Abbey Gardens, which lie beyond the impressive Abbey Gate and Norman Tower. Here paths meander past stunning floral displays in magnificent formal gardens.

Angel Hill has connections with Charles Dickens, as the famous author once stayed at the Georgian Angel Hotel, a former coaching inn, and gave readings at the Athenaeum assembly rooms. Moyse's Hall, now a museum, has flint-knapped rubble walls and is the oldest house in town. Military buffs will be fascinated by the Suffolk Regiment Museum in Gibraltar Barracks where many items from the Regiment's long history may be seen. The Greene King Visitor Centre traces the history of brewing in the town and tells the story of the Greene and King families.

St Edmundbury's Cathedral has a magnificent interior and a collection of 1,000 embroidered kneelers. The addition of a new Gothic-style lantern tower was completed in 2005. The late 14th century St Mary'sChurch also has an impressive interior and boasts the longest church aisle in England. Henry VIII's sister Mary Tudor is buried in the sanctuary. Add to this pedestrianised shopping streets, a diverse range of places to eat and many interesting attractions nearby and you have an ideal location for a short break.

Places to Visit

Abbey Gardens

Off Angel Hill

Impressive gardens, floral displays and activities for all the family. There are also remains of a Benedictine Monastery with an impressive Abbey Gate and Norman Tower.

Theatre Royal

Westgate Street, IP33 1QR
☎ 01284 769505
www.theatreroyal.org
The Theatre Royal is the only surviving Regency playhouse in Britain and can be visited to take in a performance or a guided tour.

Greene King Visitor Centre

Westgate Street, IP33 1QT
☎ 01284 714297
www.greeneking.co.uk
Children under twelve are not permitted on the brewery tour.

Top: Bury Christmas Market; Bottom: Angel Hotel

The Malthouse Project
8 Elsey's Yard, Risbygate Street, IP33 3AA
☎ 01284 732550
www.themalthouseproject.co.uk
Restored 17th century Malthouse, now a Heritage Centre and a café with guided tours around the displays of artefacts found during the restoration.

Nowton Park
Nowton Road, IP29 5LU
☎ 01284 763666
Located just to the south of the town, admission is free and the park is open all year round. It consists of almost 200 acres of Suffolk countryside, landscaped over one hundred years ago in typical Victorian style with 'country estate' features.

Bury St Edmunds Art Gallery
The Market Cross, IP33 1BT

☎ 01284 762081
www.burystedmundsartgallery.org
Housed in a fine Grade I listed Robert Adam building in the centre of the town.

Moyse's Hall Museum
Cornhill, IP33 1DX
☎ 01284 706183
The museum has an eccentric collection of local history artefacts and nationally important archaeological exhibits.

Suffolk Regiment Museum
The Keep, Gibraltar Barracks, Newmarket Road, IP33 3RN
☎ 01284 752394

Attractions Nearby

Rougham Control Tower
(3 miles/4.5km)
Rougham Tower Association, The Control Tower, Rougham Industrial Estate, IP30 9XA
☎ 01359 271471
The former home of the 94th Bomb Group, displays and other information available. They tell the story of the Tower and its part in the history of the field during World War II.

Ickworth House, Park & Gardens (NT)
(3 miles/4.5km)

The Rotunda, Horringer, IP29 5QE
☎ 01284 735270
Discover a Georgian Italianate palace in an idyllic English landscape with waymarked trails in acres of parkland. Stay in style in the East Wing; it is a hotel.

Pakenham Water Mill
(6 miles/9.5km)
Mill Road, Pakenham, IP31 2NB
☎ 01284 724075
Possibly the last working water mill in Suffolk! Produces stone-ground wholemeal flour from locally grown wheat.

West Stow Country Park & Anglo-Saxon Village
(7 miles/11.5km)
Icklingham Road, West Stow, Bury St Edmunds, IP28 6HG
☎ 01284 728718
The 125-acre park and heathland nature reserve is rich in wildlife and excellent for birdwatching, with a nature trail, woods, river, lake and bird hides.

Wyken Hall Gardens & Wyken Vineyards
(9 miles/14.5km)
IP31 2DW
Signposted from A143.
☎ 01359 250240
www.wykenvineyards.co.uk
The hall is a romantic Elizabethan Manor in four acres of gardens. Treat yourself at the Leaping Hare restaurant and shop.

Lavenham Guildhall (NT)
(11 miles/17.5km)
Market Place, Lavenham, CO10 9QZ
☎ 01787 247646
This 15th century timber-framed Tudor building has a unique display of 700 years of the medieval woollen cloth trade, complete with a loom in working order. Delightful walled

gardens and teashop.

Melford Hall (NT)
(13 miles/20km)
Long Melford, Sudbury,
CO10 9AA
☎ 01787 376395 (Infoline)
Elizabethan houses, with fine panelled banqueting hall. Beatrix Potter mementoes in the room where she was a guest. There are also delightful garden and parkland walks.

Museum of East Anglian Life
(14 miles/22.5km)
Iliffe Way, Stowmarket, IP14 1DL
☎ 01449 612229
www.eastanglianlife.org.uk
Open air museum set in seventy-five acres of beautiful countryside. Many farm buildings used to display aspects of East Anglian life. Several rare breeds of farm animals.

Boat Trip
On River Stour from Sudbury. Sudbury 15 miles/24km south on A134.
Sundays, Easter–October
☎ 01787 211507

Events

Bury St Edmunds Festival
Takes place in May over two weeks. Various venues and a variety of live entertainment.
Box office ☎ 01284 769505
email: info@buryfestival.co.uk
www.buryfestival.co.uk

Ickworth House, Park & Gardens (NT)
'Last Night of the Proms'
The Rotunda, Horringer,
Bury St Edmunds, IP29 5QE
☎ 01284 735270
Mid-July

South Suffolk Show
Ampton Racecourse, nr Ingham, Bury St. Edmunds
www.southsuffolkshow.co.uk
A one-day agricultural show in

Theatre Royal

May, regarded by many as one of the leading shows of its type in the area.

Hotels & Dining
Try the local Tourist Information Centre, see Essential Contacts for details.

Something Special

The Angel Hotel
3 Angel Hill, Bury St Edmunds, IP33 1LT
☎ 01284 714000
www.theangel.co.uk
Luxury hotel in town centre, a former Georgian coaching inn.

Clarice House
Horringer Court, Horringer Road, Bury St Edmunds, IP29 5PH
☎ 01284 705550
www.claricehousegroup.co.uk
In a beautiful Jacobean mansion set in twenty acres of park and woodland. Lavish health club abuts the original house.

Maison Bleu
31 Churchgate Street,
Bury St Edmunds, IP33 1RG
☎ 01284 760623
Wonderful unconventional fish restaurant.

Pegotty's
30 Guildhall Street,
Bury St Edmunds, IP33 1QD
☎ 01284 755444
Carvery, salad bar and house specialities.

Essential Contacts

Tourist Information Centre
6 Angel Hill, Bury St Edmunds, IP33 1UZ
☎ 01284 764667
Enquire for guided walks.

Landmark Publishing gratefully acknowledge www.visit-suffolk.org.uk for the images supplied for Bury St Edmunds.

Landmark Visitors Guide: Suffolk;
ISBN: 978 184306 389 6;
£7.99

31

Cambridge, Cambridgeshire

Top – Bottom: King's College; Cambridge University; Punting in Cambridge

Getting There

By Road

From the south & London, M11 motorway. From the north, the A1 and M1, A14. From the east and west, A14.

By Rail & Bus

There are regular train services to Cambridge from most mainline stations.

There are coach/bus services to Cambridge from around the country.

Background Briefing

Cambridge, one of Britain's ancient seats of learning, is breathtakingly beautiful with its blend of striking architecture, history and tradition, and is perfect for a romantic short break. Discover colleges, medieval churches, superb museums and picturesque bridges as you stroll around the city. If you visit in February, June or July don't miss the 'bumps' rowing races on the Cam. It is possible to visit some of the Cambridge colleges although opening days need to be checked. Don't miss the stately gothic chapel at King's, Trinity's historic buildings and grounds, Queen's old hall and chapel and the tour of St John's.

Take a leisurely trip on a punt past 'The Backs' and see the college buildings and grounds from the 'most beautiful stretch of river in the world'. Panoramic views of the city can be seen from the top of the tower at the peaceful Great St Mary's Church. The Norman Church of the Holy Sepulchre is one of only four round churches in Britain, built by the Knights Templar.

Several walking tours start from the Tourist Information Centre or you can hop onto an open-top bus and listen to a commentary. Cambridge has many attractive parks and pleasant walks can be enjoyed along the river. You can walk from Magdalene Bridge by Quayside, along Jesus Green, Midsummer Common and Stourbridge Common and out into the countryside, or take a leisurely stroll to Granchester.

Cambridge is a vibrant city with cosmopolitan restaurants serving food from all around the world. As night falls Cambridge offers a ghost walk, theatres, cinemas and clubs, concerts and recitals as well as live music in pubs.

Places to Visit

The Fitzwilliam Museum

Trumpington Street, CB2 1RB

☎ 01223 332900

www.fitzmuseum.cam.ac.uk

Collections of national and international importance. The collection includes antiquities, applied arts, illuminated manuscripts, and paintings by Constable, Hogarth, and Gainsborough.

Kings College Chapel

CB2 1ST

www.kings.cam.ac.uk

The chapel is a magnificent example of Gothic architecture with a stunning fan-vaulted roof, wonderful woodcarving and 16th century stained glass plus Rubens' "Adoration of the Magi". The annual festival of "nine lessons and carols" is broadcast from here by the BBC every Christmas.

Cambridge University Botanic Garden

Bateman Street, CB2 1JF

☎ 01223 336265

The delightful garden, just south of the city centre, covers forthy acres and has more than 10,000 plant species. The beautiful landscaped setting includes a rock garden, lake, glasshouses, woodland walk and a winter garden.

Cambridge and County Folk Museum

Castle Street, CB3 0AQ

☎ 01223 355159

www.folkmuseum.org.uk

Everyday life of the people of Cambridge and its surrounding county over the last 300 years.

Kettle's Yard

Castle Street, CB4 0AQ

☎ 01223 352124

www.kettlesyard.org. uk

Kettle's Yard Gallery is a major centre for 20th century and contemporary art.

The Junction

Clifton Road CB1 7GX

☎ 01223 578000

www.junction.co.uk

Arts venue in the heart of Cambridge, offering a diverse programme of live music, club events, comedy, theatre, dance, live art and digital art.

Attractions Nearby

Anglesey Abbey & Gardens (NT)
(7 miles/11.5km)
Quy Road Lode, CB5 9EJ
☎ 01223 811200
A restored 16th century house set in ninety-eight acres of glorious landscaped gardens.

Audley End House & Gardens (EH)
(16.5 miles/26.5km)
Saffron Walden, CB11 4JF
☎ 01799 522399
An elegant Jacobean mansion set in parkland designed by 'Capability' Brown.

Imperial War Museum Duxford
(7 miles/11.5km)
Duxford, CB2 4QR
☎ 01223 835000
duxford.iwm.org.uk
Europe's premier aviation museum.

Ely Cathedral
(17.5 miles/28km)
www.cathedral.ely.anglican.org
Building of this impressive Norman Cathedral was begun in the 11th century, Ely boasts one of the longest naves in Europe.

Newmarket Racecourses
(13miles/20.5km)
Barbra Stradbroke Avenue, Newmarket, CB8 0TG
☎ 01638 663482
www.newmarketracecourses.co.uk

The National Stud
(13 miles/20.5km)
Newmarket, CB8 0XE
☎ 01638 666789
www.nationalstud.co.uk
The only thoroughbred stud in the country to open its gates to the public for guided tours.

Oliver Cromwell's House
(17.5 miles/28km)
29 St Mary's Street, Ely, CB7 4HF
☎ 01353 662062
www.ely.org.uk/tic.htm
17th century family home of Oliver Cromwell, with famous haunted bedroom.

Shepreth Wildlife Park
(8.5 miles/14km)
Willersmill Station Road, Shepreth, SG8 6PZ
www.sheprethwildlifepark.co.uk
An outstanding collection of wild and domestic animals.

Wimpole Hall, Home Farm, Gardens & Park
Arrington, Royston, SG8 0BW
☎ 01223 206000
www.wimpole.org
A magnificent 18th century country house, surrounded by formal gardens.

Hotels & Dining
Accommodation can be booked through the local Tourist Information Centre, see Essential Contacts for details.

Something Special

Hotel Felix
Whitehouse Lane, Huntingdon Road, Cambridge, CB3 0LX
☎ 01223 277977
www.hotelfelix.co.uk
Offers a refreshingly different experience to staying in the historic city of Cambridge. Contemporary in style, set in its own attractive gardens. Two AA rosette restaurant. Continental breakfast.

Cambridge Garden House
Granta Place, Mill Lane, CB2 1RT
☎ 01223 259 988
www.cambridgegardenhouse.com
Situated on the banks of the River Cam this luxury hotel has a Health and Fitness Club with heated indoor pool, sauna, steam room and solarium.

Hotel du Vin
15-19 Trumpington Street, Cambridge, CB2 1QA
A bistro set in wonderful medieval buildings.

Midsummer House
Midsummer Common, CB4 1HA
☎ 01223 369299
French Mediterranean cuisine in a handsome Victorian villa beside the River Cam.

Essential Contacts

Visitor Information Centre
Wheeler Street, Cambridge, CB2 3QB
☎ 0871 226 8006
☎ 01223 457581

River Cruises
There are many cruise and punting businesses, here is a small selection.

Camboats
☎ 0770 673 4763
www.camboats.co.uk

Riverboat Georgina
Luxury river cruise along the Cam
☎ 01223 307694
www.georgina.co.uk

Scudamore's Punting Company Ltd
Granta Place, Mill Lane, CB2 1RS
www.scudamores.com
Punts for hire.

Ghost Tours
☎ 01223 457574

Green Wheels Pedicab Tours
A twenty or forty-five minute trishaw tours.
☎ 0871 226 8006
www.camcycle.org.uk

Cambridge Corn Exchange
Wheeler Street, CB2 3QE
☎ 01223 357851
The largest entertainment venue in Cambridge.

Getting There

By Road

M2 or M20. Follow signs to the A2 or Canterbury.

By Rail & Bus

There are several train companies offering a service into Canterbury from around the country although you may have to make changes to complete your journey.

National Express run coach services throughout the day between London Victoria and Canterbury. Several tour operators operate a daily service to Canterbury.

Background Briefing

Canterbury, the cradle of English Christianity, is steeped in history and is Kent's premier tourist destination. Wander around the cobbled alleys and narrow medieval lanes to discover castles, museums, and the magnificent world-famous cathedral. The walled cathedral precinct has numerous medieval buildings each with its own story to tell. The Cathedral, St Augustine's Abbey and St Martin's Church are part of a Unesco World Heritage Site and are not to be missed.

Canterbury is a vibrant cosmopolitan city with picturesque streets replete with international restaurants, bars and an excellent range of shops. There is so much to see in the city: visit the theatre, climb the Westgate Tower for the best views, journey back into medieval times at 'The Canterbury Tales' or simply relax by the river or walk the city walls. Parts of the Norman walls still survive and can be walked as far as Dane John Gardens; there are interpretation boards along the way.

Places to Visit

Canterbury Cathedral

The Precinct, CT1 2EH
☎ 01227 762862
www.canterbury-cathedral.org

The cathedral has a long and fascinating history and is a Unesco World Heritage Site. It is one of the finest church buildings in Britain and has been a place of pilgrimage since 1170 when Thomas a Becket was murdered here. The cathedral has stunning 12th and 13th century stained glass and is rich in monuments and tombs, including those of Edward the Black Prince and King Henry IV. Guided tours are available.

St Augustine's Abbey

Longport, Canterbury, CT1 1TF
☎ 01227 767345
Foundations of the abbey church set up by St Augustine in AD598, now in ruins. Part of the Canterbury World Heritage Site.

St Martin's Church

North Holmes Road, CT1 1QJ
The oldest church in England still in use as a parish church and part of the Canterbury World Heritage Site. The tower, added in the 14th century, is built of flint and blocks of Kentish rag stone and lined internally with large blocks of chalk.

Canterbury Castle

Castle Street
☎ 01227 378100
Ruins of a Norman keep with interpretation panels and viewing areas.

Canterbury Roman Museum

Longmarket, Butchery Lane,
☎ 01227 785575
Underground museum displaying remains of Roman town house, pavement and hypocaust room. Interactive facilities.

The Canterbury Tales

St Margaret's Street, CT1 2TG
☎ 01227 479227
www.canterburytales.org.uk
Experience the sights, smells and sounds of medieval England

Eastbridge Hospital

20 High Street, CT1 2BD
☎ 01227 471688
www.eastbridgehospital.org.uk
Medieval pilgrim's hospital with undercroft, two chapels and refectory. Early 13th century painting of Christ in glory.

Museum of Canterbury

Stour Street, CT1 2NR
☎ 01227 475202
www.canterbury.gov.uk
Interactive displays reveal the story of Canterbury.

Royal Museum & Art Gallery

High Street, CT1 2RA
☎ 01227 452747
www.canterbury.gov.uk
Museum in a magnificent Victorian building. Art from Van Dyke to the present day. Wonderful ceramics and The Buffs regimental museum.

Westgate Towers Museum

St Peter's Street, CT2 8AE
☎ 01227 789576
www.canterbury.gov.uk
Guns and armaments, prison cells and murder holes in a fortified medieval gatehouse. Panoramic views from the turrets.

Left – Right: Bell Tower, Canterbury Cathedral; Timber-framed houses on the Moet; Canterbury Cathedral; Punt on the Moet in from of Castle Northern Gatehouse

Attractions Nearby

Druidstone Wildlife & Art Park

(3 miles/5km)
Honey Hill Blean, CT2 9RJ
☎ 01227 765168
www.druidstone.net
Family day out with animals, play and picnic areas, café, enchanted woodland and labyrinth walks.

Higham Park House & Gardens

(5 miles/8km)
Bridge Hill, Bridge, CT4 5BE
☎ 01227 830830
www.higham-park.co.uk
Beautiful restored Palladian house with spectacular gardens.

Howletts Wild Animal Park

(6 miles/13km)
Bekesbourne Road, Bekesbourne, CT4 5EL
☎ 01227 721286
www.totallywild.net
Numerous exotic animals in ninety acres of beautiful parkland. Restaurant, picnic areas and adventure playground.

Wingham Wildlife Park

(6 miles/13km)
Wingham, CT3 1JL
☎ 01227 720836
www.winghamwildlifepark.co.uk
Wildlife Park with tropical glass house, parrot house, pet village and adventure playground.

Events

The **Canterbury Festival** is an international Arts Festival held in October.
www.canterburyfestival.co.uk

Hotels & Dining

Try the local Tourist Information Centre, see Essential Contacts for details.

Something Special

Abode Canterbury

High Street, CT1 2RX
☎ 01227 766266
www.abodehotels.co.uk
A listed building with many original features situated within the ancient city walls, only minutes away from the stunning Canterbury Cathedral.

Magnolia House

36 Dunstans Terrace, CT2 8AX
☎ 01227 765121
www.magnoliahousecanterbury.co.uk
A charming late Georgian family guest house in a quiet residential street just ten minutes' stroll from the city centre.

Azouma

4 Church Street, St. Paul's, CT1 1NH
☎ 01227 760076
Authentic dishes from the Lebanon, Morocco, Tunisia, Syria and Turkey.

The Goods Shed

Station Road West, CT2 8AN
☎ 01227 459 153
www.thegoodsshed.net/restaurant.html
Sit on a raised platform overlooking the farmers' market. Dishes made only with ingredients from the market.

Essential Contacts

Canterbury Information Centre

12/13 Sun Street, CT1 2HX
☎ 01227 378100

Canterbury Historic River Tours

☎ 0779 053 4744
www.canterburyrivertours.co.uk
Boats leave every fifteen to twenty minutes throughout the season.

The Canterbury River Navigation Company

☎ 07816 760869
www.crnc.co.uk
Punt trips along the Stour and through the city.

Canterbury Walks

Daily guided walks from the visitor centre, opposite the cathedral. Buy tickets from visitor centre.

Gulbenkian Theatre

University of Kent, CT2 7NB
☎ 01227 769075
www.kent.ac.uk/gulbenkian

The Marlowe Theatre

The Friars, CT1 2AS
☎ 01227 787787
www.marlowetheatre.com

Top – Bottom: Carlisle looking north towards the Scottish Hills; Morpeth Court viewed from Carlisle Park, Morpeth; Sunrise in Carlisle city centre; River Eden

Getting There

By Road

M6, J43 and A69.

By Rail & Bus

Carlisle is on the west coast mainline.

There are several coach/bus companies offering a service into Carlisle although you may have to change to complete your journey.

Background Briefing

The city of Carlisle, dominating the borderlands between England and Scotland, has a remarkable history and over the centuries has seen disputes between tribes, armies and rebels. The Celts were followed by the Romans who built the famous Hadrian's Wall, now an important World Heritage Site. Many of the city's lasting monuments were established in the tempestuous Middle Ages and are situated within the town's historic quarter. Carlisle once had mighty walls but only the west walls remain; they are, however, a good example of these early defences. The castle was founded by William the Conqueror's son in 1092, and is a lasting testament to years of feuding over the Scottish border.

Carlisle Cathedral was founded in 1122 and has been battered by centuries of warfare. The Citadel, built by Henry VIII, with its 'twin drum' bastions can be seen close to the Historic Quarter. Even the Town Hall dates from 1717 and now houses the Tourist Information Centre. However, modern Carlisle is a vibrant bustling city with superb shopping, a buzzing nightlife and delightful restaurants. Carlisle is perfectly placed for exploring Hadrian's Wall Country and the Eden Valley. Away from the city, discover the exploits of the notorious Border Reivers or perhaps simply enjoy the peace and tranquility of the beautiful countryside. You can climb aboard the Hadrian's Wall bus or take a trip on the Settle to Carlisle railway, often described as England's most scenic railway.

Places to Visit

Carlisle Castle (EH)

Castle Way, CA3 8UR

☎ 01228 591922

William the Conqueror's son founded this magnificent castle, with its crenellated battlements and turrets, in 1092. Over the years the castle has seen sieges, skirmishes and feuds and was captured by Bonnie Prince Charlie in 1745.

Mary Queen of Scots was once imprisoned here, and today you can explore its dungeons and labyrinths, find the Licking Stones and the former prisoners' carvings. The Border and King's Own Royal Border Regimental Museum is housed in the castle.

Carlisle Cathedral

7 The Abbey, CA3 8TZ

☎ 01228 548151

www.carlislecathedral.org.uk

Carlisle's red sandstone cathedral, one of Britain's smallest, has some fine 14th century glass, and the Brougham Triptych, a magnificent 16th century carved Flemish altar-piece in St Wilfrid's Chapel. There is an interesting 14th century barrel-vaulted painted ceiling above the choir stalls, which date from the 15th century and have medieval carved misericords. Don't miss the treasury with its fine display of cathedral and diocesan silver and treasures.

Tullie House Museum

Tullie House Museum & Art Gallery, Castle Street, CA3 8TP

☎ 01228 618718

www.tulliehouse.co.uk

Tullie House, set in beautiful gardens, boasts many different attractions and features brought together in one impressive museum and gallery. From fine art to interactive fun, there's something for everyone.

Citadel & West Walls

Immense and impressive oval towers that dominate the southern entrance to the City. The West Tower is open to the public.

Guildhall Museum

Fisher Street

☎ 01228 534781

Housed in the upstairs rooms of the former guildhall built in 1407 of timber, tile bricks and clay.

St. Cuthbert's Church

CA3 8UF

☎ 01228 521982

There has been a church on this site dedicated to St Cuthbert since AD685. However, the present Georgian church dates from 1778. An unusual feature is the pulpit, moveable on rails, and very tall so that the Vicar could preach to the galleries. There are many interesting burials in the churchyard, including executed soldiers from Bonnie Prince Charlie's rising in 1745, and convicts from the city's gaol.

The nearby Tythe Barn, now the Church Hall, was built sometime between 1485 and 1507.

Attractions Nearby

Birdoswald Roman Fort (EH)
(3 miles/5km)
Hadrian's Wall, CA8 7DD
☎ 01697 747602
Birdoswald is located in one of the most picturesque settings overlooking the River Irthing gorge. A Roman fort, turret and milecastle can all be seen on this excellent stretch of the Wall. A Visitor Centre brings to life the fascinating history of Birdoswald.

Lanercost Priory (EH)
3 miles north east of Brampton at Lanercos, CA8 2HQ
☎ 01697 73030
An Augustinian priory standing close to Hadrian's Wall whose beautiful 13th century church is remarkably well preserved.

Talkin Tarn Country Park
(11.5 miles/18.5km)
Talkin Brampton CA8 1HN
☎ 01697 73129
This stunning sixty-five-acre glacial tarn can be found east of Carlisle. There is a 1.3 mile woodland walk, rowing boats for hire, a play area and tea room.

A World in Miniature Museum
(4 miles/6.5km)

Left: Cross Stone in churchyard, Grinsdale; **Right:** Carlisle Cathedral

Houghton Hall, Garden Centre, Houghton, CA6 4JB.
☎ 01228 400388
www.aworldinminiature.com

Hotels & Dining
Try the Tourist Information Centre, see Essential Contacts for details.

Something Special

Best Western Cumbria Park Hotel
32 Scotland Road, Stanwix, Carlisle, CA3 9DG
☎ 01228 522887
www.bw-cumbriaparkhotel.co.uk
Victorian terrace hotel just one mile from the city centre with award-winning gardens. Leisure facilities include sauna, steam room, jacuzzi and gym.

The Crown Hotel
Wetheral, CA4 8ES
☎ 01228 561888
www.crownhotelwetheral.co.uk
The Crown Hotel is located just five miles away from the centre of Carlisle and has luxurious accommodation including some four-poster rooms.

Landmark Trust
Coop House, Netherby Summerhouse built 1760-70s. Sleeps three. Situated on bank of River Esk in isolated spot.

Farlam Hall Hotel
Brampton, CA8 2NG
☎ 016977046234
www.farlamhall.co.uk
Elegant country house hotel.

No 10 Restaurant
10 Eden Mount, CA3 9LY.
☎ 01228 524183
Good food and warm atmosphere.

Kuba
2 Crosby Street, CA1 1DQ
☎ 01228 514134
Mediterranean food.

Essential Contacts

Tourist Information Centre
Old Town Hall, CA3 8JE
☎ 01228 625 600
email: tourism@carlisle-city.gov.uk

Open Book Visitor Guiding
☎ 01228 670578

Carlisle Racecourse
Durdar Road, CA2 4TS
☎ 01228 554700
www.carlisle-races.co.uk

Hadrian's Wall, by Bus
Jump aboard to explore Hadrian's Wall. Enquire at Tourist Information or www.hadrians-wall.org

> **Landmark Visitor Guide: Lake District**
> **ISBN: 9781843063070;**
> **£9.99**

Chester, Cheshire

Getting There

By Road

From the north M6 to J20A, M56 & M53; from the south M6 to J16, A500 to Nantwich, A51 & A49 to Chester.

By Rail & Bus

There are mainline trains calling into Chester Railway Station.

There are coach/bus operators offering a service to Chester City Centre bus station from around the country although you may have to make changes to complete your journey.

Left: Tudor style shop; **Right Top:** Chester Town Hall; **Right Bottom:** Chester Cathedral

Background Briefing

Chester, originally the Roman fortress of Deva, is a major tourist attraction where half-timbered Tudor buildings, medieval streets and Georgian red brick houses vie for the visitor's attention. The red sandstone city walls are the most complete in Britain and a walk around their two mile circuit will reveal the Eastgate clock and the two-tier medieval galleries, with superb shops, known as the Rows. The city bristles with historic

Foregate Street Clock

38

buildings; the Roman amphitheatre can still be seen and a visit to the cathedral is a must. The Cloisters and Church form one of the most complete medieval monastic complexes in the country.

The Norman Castle, rebuilt in 1810, now houses the Cheshire Military Museum. Experience the sights, sounds and smells of Roman Chester at the Dewa Roman Experience or follow the city timeline at the Grosvenor Museum and take an historical journey into Chester's rich past. By walking sections of the Millennium Trail you can discover much of the city's history; the complete trail includes forty outstanding examples of Chester's architectural development. Alternatively take one of several guided walking tours offering fascinating insights into different aspects of Chester's past.

Pleasant riverside walks can be enjoyed by following the Groves Riverside Promenade Trail along the banks of the Dee. Enjoy a flutter at the Roodee, Chester's historic racecourse, or simply browse around the many shops. Chester is well known as a major retail centre and also has a huge variety of pubs, cafes, restaurants and evening entertainment.

Places to Visit

Chester Cathedral

St Werburgh Street, CH1 2HU

☎ 01244 324756

www.chestercathedral.com

First founded as a Benedictine Monastery dedicated to St Werburgh in 1092 which was disbanded following the dissolution of the monasteries. It was rededicated as the Cathedral Church of Christ and the Blessed Virgin Mary in Chester. There is a lot to see in the cathedral, both inside and outside, so take an hour to look around. Don't miss the magnificent 12th century wood-carving in the choir stalls.

The Dewa Roman Experience

Pierpoint Lane, off Bridge Street, CH1 1NL

☎ 01244 343407

www.dewaromanexperience. co.uk

The actual Dewa Roman fortress is now buried under modern-day Chester, but you can get an impression of what life was like there by visiting this attraction. The visit begins in the dark hold of a Roman galley and continues through reconstructed street scenes where you can experience the sights, sounds and smells of Roman Chester.

Cheshire Military Museum
The Castle, CH1 2DN
☎ 01244 327617
www.chester.ac.uk/militarymuseum/

Chester Racecourse
The Roodee, CH1 2LY
☎ 01244 304600
www.chester-races.co.uk

Grosvenor Museum
27 Grosvenor Street, CH1 2DD
☎ 01244 402008
www.grosvenormuseum.co.uk

Attractions Nearby

Blue Planet Aquarium
(7 miles/11km)
Cheshire Oaks, Ellesmere Port, CH65 9LF
☎ 0151 357 8800
www.blueplanetaquarium.com

Chester Zoo
(3 miles/5km)
Cedar House, Caughall Road, Upton-by-Chester, CH2 1LH
☎ 01244 380 280
www.chesterzoo.org

Ellesmere Port Boat Museum
(8 miles/13km)
South Pier Road, Ellesmere Port, CH65 4FW
☎ 0151 355 5017
www.boatmuseum.org.uk

Hotels & Dining
Book through Visit Chester. Online www.visitchester.co.uk or call the

Old English, gothic style, terraced house, built and designed by the famous architect John Douglas

Chester city centre

accommodation services team on:
☎ 0845 073 1324.

Mill Hotel & Spa
Milton Street, CH1 3NF
☎ 01244 350035
The Mill Hotel & Spa is located alongside the Shropshire Union Canal and has an exceptional health and beauty spa.

The Chester Grosvenor & Spa
Eastgate, CH1 1LT
☎ 01244 324024
www.chestergrosvenor.com
Located in the heart of the historic city, this five-star hotel, in a building dating back to 1865, has a luxury spa offering traditional and holistic treatments.

The Grosvenor-Pulford Hotel
(5 miles/8km)
Wrexham Road, Pulford, CH4 9DG
☎ 01244 570560
www.grosvenorpulfordhotel.co.uk

Rossett Hall Hotel
(10 miles/16.5km)
Chester Road, Rossett, LL12 0DE
www.rossetthallhotel.co.uk

Llyndir Hall Hotel
(8 miles/13.5km)
Llyndir Lane, Rossett, LL12 0AY
☎ 01244 571 648
www.feathers.uk.com

The Arkle Restaurant
Grosvenor Hotel, Eastgate,

CH1 1 LT
☎ 01244 895618
Michelin-starred gourmet restaurant.

Essential Contacts

Tourist Information Centre
Town Hall, Northgate Street, CH1 2HJ
☎ 01244 402111

Chester Visitor Centre
Vicar's Lane, CH1 1QX
☎ 01244 402111

Chester Boats
Souters Lane, The Groves, CH1 2SD
☎ 01244 325394
www.chesterboat.co.uk
Boat trips along the River Dee.

Chester Heritage Tours
Chester
☎ 0870 765 6840
email: info@chesterheritagetours.co.uk
www.chesterheritagetours.co.uk
Vintage bus tours of Chester.

Punch and Judy board

Lighthouse at Cromer

Getting There

By Road

From east King's Lynn – A148; from south Norwich – A140.

By Rail & Bus

Cromer is on a branch rail line from Norwich.

There are coach/bus services to Norwich. You will have to take a local bus to Cromer.

Background Briefing

Cromer with its cliff top setting overlooking pristine sands is a delightful place to visit. The beach has a Blue Flag award, gardens border the promenade and the Victorian pier boasts the Pavilion Theatre as well as a modern lifeboat station. Situated at the end of the promenade is the fascinating RNLI Henry Blogg Museum which tells the story of the RNLI's most decorated lifeboat man. Blogg was awarded three Gold and four Silver medals for gallantry, as well as the George Cross and British Empire Medal.

Fishing is a popular activity with both visitors and locals and you can still watch the crab boats arrive every morning with their catch. The handsome church of St Peter and St Paul dominates the town; its tower is thought to be the tallest in Norfolk. A climb up the 172 steps to the top of the tower is rewarded by amazing views. Adjacent to the church is the museum, occupying a row of fishermen's cottages, where it is possible to discover what life was like here in the 19th century. The museum also has picture and geology galleries. Children will appreciate Kiddieland Fun Park on the seafront where they will find a range of rides, a helter skelter and, of course, candy floss! A popular family venue is the boating lake where canoes and paddleboats are available as well as trampolines and mini golf. At the Sticky Earth Ceramic Cafe you can design, create and paint onto ceramics. A bracing cliff top walk can be enjoyed to Overstrand, one and a half miles away, passing the lighthouse and the Royal Cromer Golf Course en route. Cromer has a shopping centre, a cinema and numerous places to eat. There are many coastal villages to explore both to the west and southeast.

Places to Visit

Henry Blogg Museum

The Rocket House, The Gangway, NR27 9ET
☎ 01263 511294
www.rnli.org.uk/HenryBlogg
RNLI Coxswain; three times Gold medal winner. One of the bravest men ever to put to sea.

Church Street Gallery

3 Church Street, NR27 9ER
☎ 01263 510100
www.churchstreetgallery.co.uk
Art and studio crafts gallery.

Cromer Boating Lake

Prince of Wales Road, NR27 9HR
www.cromerboatinglake.co.uk
A range of different boats, crazy golf, 18-hole putting course and trampolines. Open Easter to September, check website for more details.

Cromer Museum

East Cottages, Tucker Street, NR27 9HB
☎ 01263 513543
Includes a recreated Victorian fisherman's cottage; exhibits on Cromer in Victorian times and Henry Blogg and the Cromer lifeboat men.

Sticky Earth Ceramic Cafe

15 Church Street, NR27 9ES
☎ 01263 519 642
www.stickyearthcafe.co.uk
A cafe where you can design, create and paint onto ceramics in a spacious, friendly and relaxed atmosphere.

Cromer Pier & the Pavilion Theatre

The Promenade, NR27 9HE
☎ 01263 512495
www.cromer-pier.com
Seaside shows and entertainment.

Attractions Nearby

Hillside Animal Sanctuary

(3 miles/5km)
Off Sandy Lane, West Runton, NR27 9QH
www.hillside.org.uk
On the site of a former Shire Horse Centre, and still has the horses.

Felbrigg Hall (NT)

(3 miles/5km)
Felbrigg Hall, Garden and Park, Felbrigg, NR11 8PR

☎ 01263 837444

One of the most elegant country houses in East Anglia with a fine Georgian interior. Stunning walled garden, orangery and orchards and trails to explore.

Priory Maze & Gardens

(3.5 miles/6km)
Cromer Road, Beeston Regis, Sheringham, NR26 8SF
☎ 01263 822986
www.priorymazegardens.com
Enchanting gardens and traditional hedge maze.

Events

Cromer Carnival

Hotels & Dining

Try the local Tourist Information Centre, see Essential Contacts for details.

Something Special

Incleborough House

(1 mile from Cromer)
Lower Common, East Runton,
☎ 01263 515939
www.incleboroughhouse.com
In a 17th century Grade II listed building and set in a magnificent half acre of secluded mature English walled garden overlooking the village green.

Cliftonville Hotel

Seafront, 29 Runton Road, Cromer, NR27 9AS
☎ 01263 512543
www.cliftonvillehotel.co.uk
Combines Edwardian elegance with modern comforts.

The Courtyard Restaurant

Wellington Mews, New Street, Cromer, NR 27 9HP
☎ 01263 515419
Fine English and International cuisine for the vegetarian.

Top: Cromer pier from the east beach; Right Top – Bottom: Corner of Garden Street, High Street and New Street; Hotel de Paris from the pier; Brunswick Terrace from the gangway; Left Top – Bottom: Looking towards the High Street from Church Street; Cromer Church

Bolton's Bistro

Cliftonville Hotel, Seafront, Cromer
☎ 01263 512543
Specialising in fresh fish dishes.

Essential Contacts

Tourist Information Centre

Prince of Wales Road, NR27 9HS
☎ 0871 200 3071

Landmark Visitor Guide: Norfolk and the Broads
ISBN: 9781843063278; £7.99

Top Left – Right: Durham Cathedral and the River Wear; Skull and frame at Durham Cathedral; Bottom Left – Right: Durham Castle; River Tees; Teesdale farmhouse

Getting There

By Road

Durham lies just off the A1(M) J62 from north or south.

By Rail & Bus

Durham railway station is on the East Coast Main Line and is well serviced by the National Rail Network.

There are several coach/bus operators offering services from around the country although you may have to change to complete your journey.

Background Briefing

Durham is an inspiring city and has one of the most beautiful and unspoilt medieval city centres to be found anywhere in northern Europe. Its iconic cathedral is well known as one of the finest examples of Romanesque architecture in the world. Today the cathedral and the castle are one of Britain's World Heritage Sites. Durham is also a

prestigious centre of education and its university is the third oldest in the country. A walk through Durham's winding streets and narrow, atmospheric alleyways will reveal much of the city's medieval heritage.

In Durham history is all around you; the Guildhall in the Market Place is an ancient building first built in 1356 and then rebuilt in 1535 and 1665; the cafe on Palace Green is in former 17th century almshouses; and the 19th century Town Hall in the Market Place is modelled on London's Westminster Hall. It has an impressive hammer-beam roof as well as superb stained glass windows and a magnificent fireplace of local stone.

Pick up a leaflet from the TIC and take a self-guided walk around the city visiting the Market Place, medieval churches, houses and bridges, alleyways, the cathedral, castle, Palace Green, university buildings, cobbled streets and the riverside. The beautiful Elvet Bridge, over the River Wear, had a chapel at each end in

the 13th century. The west chapel was replaced by the House of Correction, parts of which can still be seen. Stand on the bridge and marvel at the scenery, watch the rowers or perhaps be tempted to take a cruise on the Prince Bishop.

Wharton Park in the city centre is also a place to relax and enjoy impressive floral displays and breathtaking views of the city. Durham has an interesting juxtaposition of history and modernity; modern designer boutiques, cosmopolitan restaurants, historic pubs and delicious delicatessens in the traffic-free shopping area complement the historic streets and Victorian indoor market. Durham is also a traditional market town, and the attractive cobbled Market Place is the setting for a weekly Saturday market. Additionally, a monthly farmers' market sells local produce and craftwork on the third Thursday of each month. Durham is an ideal touring base and there are many attractions in the area as well as simply stunning scenery.

Places to Visit

Durham Castle
West Rainton, Houghton Le Spring

The castle is contemporary with the cathedral and was the seat of the Prince Bishops until 1832. This former Norman fortress now houses University College, the foundation college of Durham University, and is open for guided tours.

Durham Cathedral
The College, DH1 3EH
☎ 0191 384 1690
www.durhamcathedral.co.uk

The Cathedral has an incomparable setting, build on a peninsula of land in a loop of the River Wear. The cathedral, well known as the best-preserved Norman structure in Europe, was built over forty years starting in 1093. The tombs of St Cuthbert and the Venerable Bede can be seen inside together with stone rib vaulting, stained glass windows, wall paintings, zigzag arches, the Bishop's throne and Prior Castell's Clock. In fact from the moment of entering by the north door, with its great bronze sanctuary knocker, the visitor is spellbound by the glorious grandeur and awe-inspiring splendour of this wonderful building.

Above: Durham Castle   Below: Birds on driftwood in the weir in Durham

Durham University Botanic Garden
Hollingside Lane, South Road, DH1 3TN
☎ 0191 3345521
www.dur.ac.uk/botanic.garden

An eighteen acre garden set among beautiful mature woodlands on the southern outskirts of Durham. The garden has a tropical house, cactus house and Prince Bishop's Garden. There is also a visitor centre with changing exhibitions and a cafe.

Durham Light Infantry Museum & Durham Art Gallery
Aykley Heads, DH1 5TU
☎ 0191 3842214
www.durham.gov.uk/dli

Set in beautiful gardens, on the

edge of the city, and built on the site of the last working colliery in Durham.

Durham Heritage Centre
St Mary-le-Bow, North Bailey, DH1 3ET
☎ 0191 384 5589
www.durhamheritagecentre.org.uk

Museum of Local History
Telling the story of Durham, from medieval times to the present day. Exhibitions, models, hands-on activities, brass rubbing and videos.

Houghall Gardens
East Durham and Houghall College, Stockton Road
www.durhamtourism.co.uk

Houghall Gardens are located just outside the centre of Durham. There are displays of gardening styles from formal beds to a water garden, arboretum and woodland garden.

Views around Durham Cathedral and its cloisters

43

Old Fulling Mill Museum of Archaeology
The Banks, DH1 3EB
☎ 0191 334 1823
www.dur.ac.uk/fulling.mill
An archaeological museum illustrating the history of Durham.

St Nicholas' Church
Market Place, DH1 1JP
☎ 0191 384 1180
www.stnics.org.uk
Originally a Norman church whose north wall once continued the city wall.

Oriental Museum
Elvet Hill DH1 3TH
☎ 0191 334 5694
www.dur.ac.uk/oriental.museum
The only museum in the country devoted entirely to Oriental art and antiquities.

Crook Hall & Gardens
Frankland Lane, Sidegate, DH1 5SZ
☎ 0191 384 8028
www.crookhallgardens.co.uk
Within walking distance of the city centre, and comprising of a medieval manor house and delightful English gardens.

Attractions Nearby

Auckland Castle
(11 miles/18km)
Bishop Auckland, DL14 7NR
☎ 01388 601627
www.auckland-castle.co.uk
Auckland Castle is the home of the Bishop of Durham, and has been for the past 800 years.

Beamish
(12.5 miles/20km)
The North of England Open Air Museum, Beamish, DH9 0RG
☎ 0191 3704000
www.beamish.org.uk
This is no ordinary museum but a living, working experience of life as it was in the Great North in the early 1800s and 1900s.

Sedgefield Racecourse
(15 miles/24.5km)
Stockton-on-Tees, TS21 2HW
☎ 01740 621925
www.sedgefield-racecourse.co.uk

Durham County Cricket Club
(10 miles/16km)
County Ground, Riverside, Chester-le-Street, DH3 3QR
☎ 0191 387 1717
www.durhamccc.co.uk

Washington Old Hall (NT)
(12 miles/19.5km)
The Avenue, Washington Village, Washington, NE38 7LE
☎ 0191 416 6879
Ancestral home of George Washington.

Events

Miners' Gala

Durham Regatta

Durham Literature Festival

Durham International Festival

Hotels & Dining

Accommodation can be booked through the local Tourist Information Centre, see Essential Contacts for details.

Something Special

The Royal County Hotel
Old Elvet, DH1 3JN
☎ 0118 971 4700
www.marriott.co.uk
The four star Royal County Hotel in Durham occupies a prime location on the banks of the River Wear in the heart of Durham's historic city centre.

Ramside Hall Hotel & Golf Club
Carrville, Durham, DH1 1TD
☎ 0191 386 5282

email: mail@ramsidehallhotel.co.uk
Formerly the home of the Pemberton family, Ramside Hall was transformed into a hotel in 1963. Located some two miles from Durham.

Landmark Trust
The Banqueting House, Gibside, nr Newcastle upon Tyne
Built in 1746, The Banqueting House has considerable 'wow' factor. around fourteen miles from Durham. Sleeps four.

Gourmet Spot
The Avenue, DH1 4DX
☎ 0191 384 6655
www.gourmet-spot.co.uk
Durham's boldest fine dining restaurant.

Oldfields Restaurant
18 Claypath, DH1 1RH
☎ 0191 3709595
www.oldfieldsrestaurants.com
Award winning restaurant serving great British food.

Essential Contacts

Tourist Information Centre
Millennium Place, DH1 1WA
☎ 0191 3843720
www.durhamtourism.co.uk

Gala Theatre & Cinema
Millennium Place, DH1 1WA
☎ 0191 332 4041

Prince Bishop River Cruiser
The Boathouse, Elvet Bridge, DH1 3AF
☎ 0191 386 9525

Cathedral Bus
www.durham.gov.uk
A search for Cathedral Bus will give the timetable etc. The Cathedral Bus Service links the Cathedral, Rail Station and car & coach parks.

Exeter, Devon

Above: Mols Coffee House; **Below:** Exeter Cathedral

Getting There

By Road

M5 or from M3, J8 then A303/A30.

By Rail & Bus

There are mainline services into Exeter Central Station from around the country.

Most coach/bus operators offer a service into Exeter but you may have to make changes to complete your journey.

Background Briefing

Exeter, a charming capital city in the heart of Devon, is ideally located near to coast and countryside. The city owes its past wealth to the woollen cloth industry which once flourished in the area. The imposing Custom House, built in 1680, housed the officials who collected taxes on traded goods and is the city's oldest brick building. Although largely rebuilt after the bombing in World War II, Exeter still has many reminders of past glories. The White Hart Hotel dates from the 14th century and parts of the Roman wall, which once encircled the city, can still be seen.

The present Guildhall is a product of the late 15th century and has a timber framed roof whose timbers are supported on stone corbels carved to resemble grotesque animals. The close of the magnificent Norman cathedral contains a miscellany of period architecture. The cathedral itself has wonderful medieval stained glass and an awe-inspiring vaulted ceiling. A good way to explore the city is to pick up one of the self-guided trail leaflets from the tourist office; why not walk the city walls or follow the Woollen Trail.

There is an opportunity to go underground to explore Exeter's 14th century tunnels where you are taken through narrow passageways built to house the pipes that brought fresh water to the city. Just off the High Street are Northernhay Gardens and Rougemont Gardens which together incorporate the oldest public space in England. The gardens contain the remains of Rougemont Castle and sections of the town's Roman and Saxon walls.

Exeter's historic quayside is an attractive area with interesting 19th century warehouses, antique and craft shops and lively places to eat. It's a pleasant place to simply stroll or to take a relaxing boat trip. The more energetic can hire a cycle and ride alongside the picturesque canal. Exeter has something for everyone: history, heritage and superb shopping, including a popular Farmers' Market held every Thursday and the Slow Food Market, located on the historic Quayside, which is held on the third Saturday each month.

Places to Visit

Exeter Cathedral

1 The Cloisters, EX1 1HS
☎ 01392 214219
www.exeter-cathedral.org.uk
Exeter's majestic Cathedral is over 850 years old and one of the finest examples of the Decorated Gothic style in England. There is wonderful stained glass, a sixty-foot high oak Bishop's throne, a minstrel's gallery and the brightly decorated Angel Gabriel's Chapel. The Cathedral's west front is adorned with magnificent sculptured figures depicting saints, kings and angels.

Above Top – Bottom: Castle; Ancient church surrounded by shops; Killerton; Killerton
Left: City centre shoppers

Exeter's Underground Passageways

2 Paris Street, EX1 1GA
☎ 01392 665887
www.exeter.gov.uk
Explore the interpretation centre, which allows you to fly through the passages on a magic carpet! There is an introductory film, hands on exhibits and a guided tour through the passages.

The Quay House Visitor Centre

46 The Quay, EX2 4AN
☎ 01392 265213
The Visitor Centre is housed in a former 17th century warehouse and provides an exciting audio-visual history of Exeter together with models and items from the cloth industry.

Topsham

This beautiful town, on the Exe estuary, is still a part of Exeter and a perfect place to enjoy river walks or simply watch the sailing boats. The atmospheric streets have some interesting architecture, unusual shops, ancient hostelries and fine restaurants. There is also a museum if you wish to learn more of Topsham's history.

Connections Discovery Centre

Rougemont House, Castle Street, EX4 3PU
☎ 01392 265360
An interesting and interactive look into Exeter's past.

St Nicolas Priory

The Mint, Off Fore Street, EX4 3BL
☎ 01392 665858
This fascinating building was formerly the guest wing of a 900 year old Benedictine priory.
It is one of Exeter's hidden jewels and recently reopened its doors after a two-year refurbishment. The priory has been furnished as an Elizabethan town house where visitors can experience Tudor life.

Attractions Nearby

The Exe Estuary
An important wildlife centre best explored on foot or bicycle. More sedentary visitors can see the area on a scenic boat cruise or a guided RSPB wildlife cruise.

Castle Drogo (NT)
(21 miles/40km)
Drewsteignton, nr Exeter,
EX6 6PB
☎ 01647 433306
Perched high above the Teign Gorge this is one of the most remarkable works of Sir Edwin Lutyens and the last castle to be built in England.

A La Ronde (NT)
(14 miles/22km)
Summer Lane, Exmouth,
EX8 5BD
☎ 01395 265514
A unique sixteen-sided, 18th-century house with stunning panoramic views over the Exe Estuary.

Killerton (NT)
(8 miles/12.5km)
Broadclyst, Exeter, EX5 3LE
☎ 01392 881345
Fine 18th century house with costume collection, hillside garden and estate. The surrounding parkland and woods offer beautiful circular walks. Also Budlake Old Post Office Room, a 1950s PO with cottage garden, and Clyston Mill, a water-powered grain mill in working order.

Hotels & Dining

Book through local Tourist Information Centre, see Essential Contacts for details.

Something Special

Buckerell Lodge Hotel
Topsham Road, EX2 4SQ
☎ 01392 221111
www.foliohotels.com/

buckerelllodge
Located just outside Exeter in its own extensive grounds.

Woodbury Park Hotel, Golf and Country Club
(9 and a half miles from Exeter)
Woodbury Castle, Woodbury,
Exeter, EX5 1JJ
☎ 01395 233382
www.woodburypark.co.uk
Luxurious hotel set in acres of beautiful countryside with two golf courses, fitness studio, fully equipped gym, pool, sauna and jacuzzi.

Thistle Hotel
Queen Street, EX4 3SP
☎ 0871 3769018
Good location in the heart of the city.

Abode
Cathedral Yard, EX1 1HD
☎ 01392 319955
email: reservationsexeter@
abodehotels.co.uk
www.abodehotels.co.uk
Absolute luxury, fine dining, resident's gym and beauty treatments.

The Galley Fish and Seafood Restaurant
41 Fore Street, Topsham,
EX3 0HU
☎ 01392 876078
www.galleyrestaurant.co.uk

Red Square Restaurant
Rougemont House, Castle Street,
EX4 3PU
☎ 01392 411292
www.redsquarerestaurant.co.uk
Authentic Russian cuisine served in an 18th century building in a secluded spot.

Exeter Phoenix
Bradninch Place, Gandy Street,
Ex4 3LS
☎ 01392 667080
www.exeterphoenix.org.uk
Contemporary programme of

dance, theatre, live art, etc.

The Northcott Theatre
Stocker Road, EX4 4QB
☎ 01392 493493
www.exeternorthcott.co.uk

Exeter Corn Exchange
George St, EX1 1BU
01392 665866
www.exeter.gov.uk/
cornexchange
Entertainment venue.

Events

The Exeter Festival of South West England
Food and drink. Takes place in March/April.

Exeter Summer Festival

Exeter Autumn Festival
www.efestivals.co.uk
☎ 01392 265700 for festival details.

Exeter Red Coat Guided Tours
Exeter Visitor Information & Tickets, Dixs Field, Exeter,
EX1 1JJ
☎ 01392 265203
Fascinating free tours around the city.

Boat Trips
Exeter Cruises
www.exetercruises.com
☎ 07984 368442

Essential Contacts

Tourist Information Centre
Civic Centre, Paris Street,
EX1 1NN
☎ 01392 265700
email tic@exeter.gov.uk

Landmark Visitors
Guide: Devon;
ISBN: 9781843063735;
£9.99

Gloucester, Gloucestershire

Top – Bottom: The tiny house of Beatrix Potter's Tailor of Gloucester; Farmers' Market; Gloucester Cathedral

Getting there

By Road

M5 south, J11 A40; north, J12 or 11a.

By Rail & Bus

There are rail services into Gloucester Rail Station from around the country although you may have to make changes to complete your journey.

There are bus/coach services into Gloucester from around the country.

Background Briefing

Gloucester was once an important Roman town known as Glevum; parts of the Roman walls remain and excavations of Roman Eastgate can be seen below street level in Eastgate Street. Gloucester, overlooked by the Cotswold Hills and formerly the largest inland port in Britain, has a vibrant city centre, a magnificent Norman cathedral and a fascinating dock area full of interesting and unusual museums. The docks have a number of restored Victorian warehouses now housing award-winning museums, a huge antiques centre, cafes and shops. The waterfront is a pleasant place where visitors will see all kinds of vessels and can take the opportunity to take a trip on a pleasure craft. The National Waterways Museum brings the history of our inland waterways to life. This child-friendly museum has hands-on exhibits, interactive facilities and historic canal boats to explore.

The Soldiers of Gloucestershire Museum, located in the Custom House, tells the story of local regiments with the help of life-size displays, sound effects, computer games and film archives. A short walk away from the cathedral, down narrow, cobbled streets, is the main pedestrianised shopping centre. An award-winning Farmers' Market is held in the city centre, around the Cross, every Friday. Gloucester has a range of restaurants catering for truly global tastes but why not try a Gloucester Old Spot Sausage or try Cats Whiskers, Grim Reaper and Cotswold, all beers from Gloucester breweries. The city is also an ideal base to stay while touring the surrounding Cotswold countryside and the Forest of Dean.

Places to Visit

Gloucester Cathedral

2 College Green, GL1 2LR
www.gloucestercathedral.org.uk
John Betjeman once described Gloucester Cathedral as 'Northern Europe's sixth most beautiful building' and certainly the cathedral with its magnificent fan vaulted cloisters and great east window has varied stunning architecture including Romanesque and early Perpendicular. The Norman lead font dates from around 1137 and has seated figures and foliage. Throughout the cathedral are forty Green Men, dating from the Middle Ages, including some quite unlike any found in other English churches. The choir has fine misericords beneath the stall seats and the roof has a carved Angel Orchestra. Don't miss the Great Cloister, with its fine fan vaulting. It was used for the corridor scenes at Hogwarts in the Harry Potter movies. A memorial to Bishop Hoper can be seen opposite the cathedral. He was burnt at the stake here in 1555 for being a Lutheran.

National Waterways Museum

Llanthony Warehouse, Gloucester, Docks GL1 2EH
☎ 01452 318200
Recently refurbished, this fascinating museum has new exhibits. 'Water Lives' draws on the experiences of real people who worked on the canals. The wildlife that exists along canals and rivers will be featured in the 'Ecology Gallery' and the interactive 'Move It' will explain how the canals were built and operated.

Blackfriars (EH)

Blackfriars Lane
One of the most complete surviving friaries of the Dominican 'black friars' in England, later converted into a Tudor house and cloth factory. Notable features include the church and the fine scissor-braced dormitory roof.

City Museum & Art Gallery

Brunswick Road, Gl1 1HP
☎ 01452 396131
Items of national and international importance with something of interest for everyone.

Gloucester Folk Museum

99–103 Westgate Street, GL1 2PG
☎ 01452 396467
Three floors of history in the oldest timber framed buildings in the city. Discover the history of domestic life, crafts, trades and industries from

the 1500s to the present day.

Gloucester Antiques Centre
1 Severn Road, The Docks, GL1 2LE
☎ 01452 529716
Over 140 antique dealers who trade in a converted grain warehouse.

House of the Tailor of Gloucester
9 College Court, GL1 2HJ
☎ 01452 422856
Charming shop and museum in the original building used by Beatrix Potter in 'The Tailor of Gloucester'.

St James City Farm
23 Albany Street, GL1 4NG
☎ 01452 305728
Rare breeds of sheep, goats, pigs and poultry.

The Soldiers of Gloucestershire Museum
Custom House, Gloucester Docks GL1 2HE
☎ 01452 522682
This award-winning museum tells the story of the county's soldiers and their families in peacetime and war during the last 300 years.

Attractions Nearby

Clearwell Caves
(21 miles/34km)
The Rocks, Clearwell, Coleford, GL16 8JR
Nine large caverns in a superb natural cave system mined for iron ore and ochre pigment for over 4,500 years.

Puzzle Wood
(20.5 miles/33km)
Coleford, GL16 8QD
A mile of pathways winding through fourteen acres of scenic ancient woodland. Wander through deep ravines and over wooden bridges, through moss-covered rocks and between ancient trees. The paths were laid to form an unusual maze.

Dean Heritage Centre
(15.5 miles/25km)
Camp Mill, Soudley, Cinderford, GL14 2UB
Imaginative galleries housed in a former corn mill tell the story of the Dean (Forest of Dean) and its people.

Nature In Art
(3.5 miles/6km)
Wallsworth Hall, Twigworth, GL2 9PA
☎ 01452 731422
Housed in a Georgian mansion is the world's first museum dedicated to art inspired by nature.

Robinswood Hill Country Park
(2.5 miles/4km)
Reservoir Road, GL4 6SX
☎ 01452 304779
Set in 250 acres of countryside offering pleasant walks & views. Waymarked nature, geology & horse trails, and a guided walks programme is also available. Rare breeds farm.

Westbury Court Garden
(9.5 miles/15km)
Westbury-on-Severn, GL14 1PD
☎ 01452 760461
www.nationaltrust.org.uk
The only restored Dutch water garden in the country. Reputedly home to England's oldest evergreen oak with many other 16th and 17th-century trees and shrubs.

Hotels & Dining
Try the local Tourist Information Centre, see Essential Contacts for details.

Something Special

Hatherley Manor Hotel
Down Hatherley Lane, GL2 9QA
☎ 01452 730217
www.hatherleymanor.com

17th century manor just four miles from Gloucester.

Ramada Bowden Hall
Bondend Lane, Upton St Leonard,
☎ 0844 8159044
www.ramadajarvis.co.uk
The Regency style Ramada Bowden Hall Gloucester hotel is set in twelve acres of woodland. The Seb Coe Health Club provides a swimming pool and sauna.

Fosters on the Docks
Kimberley Warehouse, Gloucester Docks, GL1 2ES
☎ 01452 300990
www.fostersonthedocks.com

Essential Contacts

Tourist Information Centre
28 Southgate Street, GL1 2DP
☎ 01452 396572

Gloucester Civic Trust
For hour long walking tours of the city and historic docks, also look out for the information point on Merchants Quay on the docks.
☎ 01452 396572

Gloucester Ghost Walks
28 Southgate Street, GL1 2DP
☎ 01452 396572

Boat Trips
National Waterways Museum
☎ 01452 318200
www.gloucestercruises.org.uk
For boat trips along the canal.

Landmark Publishing gratefully acknowledges Gloucester City Council for the images supplied on page 46. For further information visit: www.visitgloucester.info

Getting There

By Road

From south: via Leeds, take A61 to Harrogate or A1/A661 from Wetherby. From north; via A1(M) to J47 Knaresborough then take A59 to Harrogate.

By Rail & Bus

There are mainline trains operating into Harrogate although you may need to change to complete the journey.

There are coach/bus services into Harrogate from round the country.

Background Briefing

This genteel, elegant spa town has magnificent Victorian architecture, award-winning gardens, broad tree-lined streets and a nationally celebrated local theatre. The town has a rich spa heritage and was very popular in the 18th century when the spa water was claimed to cure all kinds of illnesses including nervous tension, gout, rheumatism and lumbago.

Harrogate has the most beautiful and complete Turkish Baths in England, complete with colourful Arabic tiles, elaborate arched roofs and oak and mahogany changing rooms.

Harrogate is well known as the antiques centre of the north and is a shopper's paradise, with Victorian streets lined with stylish stores and boutiques, and small mews full of sophisticated antique, art and gift shops. The dignified Montpelier Quarter is an ideal place to shop for unusual and unique gifts, designer clothes and works of art or to enjoy a break at the famous Betty's Tea Rooms. Additionally weekly markets are held on Thursdays and there is a monthly Farmers' Market. The town has an impressive range of cosmopolitan restaurants and wine bars, perhaps reflecting the tastes

of the many visitors to Harrogate's International Centre.

Away from the town a pleasant walk leads from the Valley Gardens, through pinewoods up to the gardens at Harlow Carr. Details of this hour-long walk can be obtained from the Tourist Information Centre. Harrogate is a charming town surrounded by the stunning countryside of the Yorkshire Dales and is an ideal base to visit nearby imposing historic houses, castles, cathedrals and abbeys. Not far away is Knaresborough where Georgian houses proliferate in a charming market town. A little further is Ripon with interesting museums and a cathedral with a Saxon crypt.

Places to Visit

Mercer Art Gallery

Swan Road, HG1 2SA
☎ 01423 556188
www.harrogate.gov.uk
The gallery is housed in Harrogate's oldest spa building, constructed as a promenade room to accommodate the large numbers of visitors coming to Harrogate to take the waters. The gallery's fine art collection consists of some 2,000 works of art, mainly from the 19th and 20th centuries.

Royal Pump Room Museum

Crown Place, HG1 2RY
☎ 01423 556188
www.harrogate.gov.uk
Sample the waters of the strongest sulphur well in Britain, and when you've recovered, discover the intriguing story of how Harrogate became a spa town.

Turkish Baths & Health Spa

Parliament Street, HG1 2WH
☎ 01423 556746
www.harrogate.gov.uk
Indulge yourself at these traditional Turkish Baths built in 1897. There are sauna and steam rooms, plus

Top – Bottom: Horn Blower; Prison & Police Museum; Boats at Knaresborough

various beauty treatments and types of massage on offer.

Valley Gardens (EH)

Between Valley Drive and Cornwall Road, HG1 2RY
☎ 01423 500600
This Grade II listed garden, famous for incredible flower displays, was first laid out between 1880–1900.

The Stray

An attractive area in the old town where there are over 200 acres of resplendent lawns used for sport, picnics, special events or just a stroll. Many of the trees are illuminated in the evenings.

Attractions Nearby

Harlow Carr Botanical Gardens

(2 miles/3.5km)
Crag Lane HG3 1QB
☎ 01423 565418
www.rhs.org.uk
The Royal Horticultural Society's most northerly gardens where you

Left – Right: Knaresborough; Shopping in Harrogate; Viaduct at Knaresborough; Royal Baths; Valley Gardens; Castle

can see spectacular gardens.

Fountains Abbey & Studley Royal Water Garden (NT)
(14 miles/22.5km)
Ripon, HG4 3DY
☎ 01765 608888
A World Heritage Site of outstanding historic and aesthetic importance. The Abbey, founded in 1132, is Britain's largest monastic ruin.

Knaresborough Castle & Museum
(4.5 miles/7.5km)
Castle Yard, Knaresborough, HG5 8AS
☎ 01423 556188
www.knaresborough.co.uk

Lightwater Valley Birds of Prey Centre
(16 miles/25.5km)
North Stainley, Ripon, HG4 3HT
☎ 01765 635010
www.lightwaterbirdsofprey.co.uk
State of the art falconry complex and home to Britain's largest golden eagle.

Ripley Castle
(3.5 miles/6.5km)
Ripley Castle Estate, Ripley, HG3 3AY
☎ 01423 770152
www.ripleycastle.co.uk

Ripon Cathedral
(11.5 miles/18.5km)
Minster Road, Ripon, HG4 1QS
☎ 01765 603462
www.riponcathedral.org.uk

Ripon Workhouse Museum
(11.5 miles/18.5km)
Allhallowgate, Ripon, HG4 1LE
☎ 01765 690799
Visit Britain's first workhouse museum which is situated in the men's casual wards of the former Ripon Union Workhouse. All children must be accompanied by an adult.

Festivals

Sunday Series
Classical coffee morning concerts.

Theakston's Old Peculier Crime Writing Festival

Harrogate International Festival
Contact TIC for further details.

Hotels & Dining
Book through Tourist Information Centre, see Essential Contacts for details.

Something Special

The Majestic Hotel
Ripon Road, HG1 2HU
☎ 01423 700300
www.paramount-hotels.co.uk
A charming and elegant Victorian hotel offering 'Bodysense Health & Leisure Club' and a wide range of innovative beauty and alternative therapies.

Swallow St George
1 Ripon Road, HG1 2SY
☎ 01423 561431
www.swallow-hotels.com
An elegant Edwardian hotel situated in the heart of Harrogate with facilities which include an indoor swimming pool, whirlpool, gymnasium, sauna and steam room. Beauty treatments are also available at the hotel.

Landmark Trust
Beamsley Hospital, nr Skipton. Founded in 1593, a circular building that sleeps five.

Quantro Restaurant
3 Royal Parade, HG1 2SZ
☎ 01423 503034
www.quantro.co.uk
Michelin-recommended and serving good local food.

La Tasca
1 John Street, HG1 1JZ
☎ 01423 566333
Spanish Tapas bar and restaurant.

Essential Contacts

Tourist Information Centre
Royal Baths, Crescent Road, HG1 2RR
☎ 0845 389 3223

Harrogate International Centre
King's Road, HG1 5LA
Box Office ☎ 0845 1308840
www.harrogateinternationalcentre.co.uk
Trade fairs, exhibitions and entertainment.

Harrogate Theatre
Oxford Street, HG1 1QF
☎ 01423 502116
www.harrogatetheatre.co.uk

Brimham Rocks

Nidderdale

Landmark Publishing gratefully acknowledges Harrogate International; for the images supplied on these two pages.

Landmark Visitors Guide: Yorkshire Dales; ISBN: 9781843063889; £9.99

Landmark Visitors Guide: Harrogate; ISBN: 9781843064282; £4.99

Top - Bottom: Ipswich Marina; Apartments on the marina

Getting There

By Road

A14 from Cambridge.
A12 from London.

By Rail & Bus

Ipswich is a mainline rail station,

There are national coach/bus services into Ipswich although you may have to make changes to complete your journey.

Background Briefing

Ipswich is one of England's oldest towns and has much to offer the visitor. Follow the Wet Dock Maritime Trail along the fascinating historic waterfront and stroll past Tudor merchants' houses, the old custom house, inns, warehouses and quays. River cruises sail past historical sites and beautiful scenery, while a well-maintained footpath along the banks of the Orwell is ideal for a gentle stroll.

John Constable often sketched scenes along the quay and Giles, the cartoonist, lived and worked in the town. The statue of Giles' cantankerous Grandma is to be found at the junction of Princes Street and the Butter Market. There are several fine buildings in the town including the 16th century Ancient House decorated with marvellous East Anglian pargeting. Also there is the timber framed Unitarian Meeting House with a gallery and box pews in its magnificent interior.

Ipswich Museum has interesting exhibitions charting the development of the town. The spectacular Victorian Town Hall houses the Town Hall Galleries, which have changing programmes of contemporary art. Christchurch Mansion is just a short walk from the town centre; this lovely Tudor mansion, set in sixty-five acres of parkland, is furnished as an English country house and has important collections of work by Gainsborough and Constable. The Wolsey Art Gallery, celebrating Thomas Wolsey's connection to the town, is attached to Christchurch Mansion. Cardinal Wolsey was born in Ipswich and you can still see Wolsey's Gate near the Waterfront.

Ipswich has several medieval churches; St Margaret's has a double hammerbeam roof to the nave and St Stephen's, which houses the Tourist Information Centre, is a delightful church. Ipswich has good pedestrianised shopping, theatres and plentiful pubs and restaurants to suit all tastes.

Places to Visit

Christchurch Mansion

Christchurch Park, Soane Street, IP4 2BE
☎ 01473 433554
Tudor mansion set in sixty-five acres with collections of work by Gainsborough and Constable.

Ipswich Museum

High Street, IP1 3QH
☎ 01473 433551
Includes several themes, from Roman Suffolk, Anglo-Saxon Ipswich and the Victorian Natural History Gallery.

Ipswich Transport Museum

Old Trolley Bus Depot, Cobham Road, IP3 9JD
☎ 01473 715666
Largest collection in the country of transport exhibits from just one area. All were made or used around Ipswich. Gift shop and tea room.

The Town Hall Galleries

Cornhill, IP1 1DH
Visit www.visualarts-ipswich.org.uk for more information.

The John Russell Gallery

4–6 Wherry Lane, IP4 1LG
☎ 01473 212051
www.artone.co.uk

Attractions Nearby

Pin Mill

(10 miles/16.5km)
IP9 1JP
A picturesque village on the banks of the Orwell, perfect for a riverside walk or a drink at the waterside pub. Head south on A137 and bear left on A1456, turn left at Chelmondiston and head for the river.

Baylham House Rare Breeds Farm

(5 miles/8km)
Mill Lane, Baylham, IP6 8LG
☎ 01473 830 264
Take the A14 north, exit J52, B1113, turn right at first junction towards Needham Market. Baylham House is off the B1113 down Mill Lane, Baylham.
Ideal for children to get up close and friendly with animals.

Woodbridge

(8 miles/13km)
Head north on the A12 and follow the signs.
Woodbridge has a tide mill and is home to the Suffolk Punch Heavy

Pykenham Gate from rear

Horse Museum. Nearby is the Sutton Hoo Burial Site.

Flatford: Bridge Cottage (NT)
(11 miles/17.5km)
East Bergholt, CO7 6UL
☎ 01206 298260
Beautiful 16th-century thatched cottage with John Constable exhibition and walks by the River Stour.

Events

Suffolk Show in May
www.suffolkshow.co.uk

Evening Entertainment

Regent Theatre
3 St. Helen's Street, IP4 1HE
☎ 01473 433100 (Box Office)
www.ipswichregent.com

The New Wolsey Theatre
Civic Drive, P1 2AS
☎ 01473 295 900 (Box Office)
www.wolseytheatre.co.uk

Tours and Travel

The Harwich Harbour Cruise & the Pin Mill Cruise
Operated by Orwell River Cruises and depart from the Wet Dock.
☎ 01473 836680

www.orwellrivercruises.com

Ipswich Buses
Circular tour of the town past landmarks and points of interest. They operate a hop on and off service.
☎ 0800 919390
www.ipswichbuses.co.uk

Hotels & Dining
Try the local Tourist Information Centre, see Essential Contacts for details.

Something Special

Clarice House
Bramford, IP8 4AZ
☎ 01473 463262
www.claricehousegroup.co.uk
Classic country houses in parkland settings offer a unique ambience, worlds apart from everyday concerns.

The Salthouse Harbour Hotel
1 Neptune Quay, IP4 1AS
☎ 01473 226789
www.salthouseharbour.co.uk
Luxury hotel in converted warehouse overlooking the marina.

Hintlesham Hall Hotel
(4 miles/6.5km)
Hintlesham, IP8 3NS
☎ 01473 652334
www.hintleshamhall.com
16th century country house set in 175 acres with fully equipped leisure club, beauty treatment suite and outdoor heated swimming pool.

Bistro on the Quay
3 Wherry Quay, IP4 1AS
☎ 01473 286677
www.bistroonthequay.co.uk
The Bistro is on the historic waterfront in a former salt warehouse.

Il Punto
Neptune Quay, IP4 1AX
☎ 01473 289748
www.ilpunto.co.uk

Top - Botom: Quayside restaurants and hotel on Ipswich Waterfront; Dial Lane; Guided walks of Ipswich with a Blue Badge Tour Guide

French brasserie. Il Punto is moored at Neptune Quay.

Essential Contacts

Tourist Information Centre
St. Stephens Church, St. Stephens Lane, Ipswich, IP1 1DP
☎ 01473 258070
email: mailto:tourist@ipswich.gov.uk
Enquire here for details of Blue Badge guided walks and Ghost Walks.

Landmark Publishing gratefully acknowledges Ipswich Borough Council for the images supplied on page 53.
www.visit-ipswich.com

King's Lynn, Norfolk

Getting there

By Road

From the west, A17 or A47; from the south the A10.

By Rail & Bus

There are mainline services into King's Lynn from around the country although it may involve changing trains to complete the journey.

There are national coach/bus services into King's Lynn from around the country although it may involve making changes.

Background Briefing

The historic medieval port of King's Lynn with its blend of Tudor, Jacobean and Flemish houses was chosen by the BBC to represent 19th century London in their production of *Martin Chuzzlewit*. Medieval churches and guildhalls, elegant merchants' houses and England's only surviving Hanseatic warehouse vie for the visitor's attention. Perhaps the most famous monument to the town's maritime prosperity is the Custom House, built in 1683 on Purfleet Quay, which houses the Tourist Information Centre and a maritime exhibition. True's Yard, the last remaining fisherman's yard, has a museum, gift

Statue of George Vancouver

shop and tearoom.

Explore everyday life in Lynn through the ages in the Town House Museum and discover the mysteries of the 4,000 year old timber circle known as Seahenge in Lynn Museum. Live entertainment is provided at the King's Lynn Corn Exchange and at the Arts Centre situated in St George's Guildhall, the oldest civic hall in England. The 12th century St Margaret's Church in the Saturday Market Place overlooks some of the finest ancient architecture in England, including the chequered flint and brick Trinity Guildhall built in the 1420s.

Greyfriar's Tower located in the attractive Tower Gardens is the last significant remaining part of a friary established in the 1230s by a group of Franciscan Friars. Marriot's Warehouse is a fine example of an old Tudor warehouse, which now houses The Green Quay, a discovery centre dedicated to the Wash and its wildlife. There is so much to explore in King's Lynn that a visit to the Tourist Information Centre is a must. Several self-guided trail leaflets are available including the Maritime Trail, highlighting twenty-five locations each with a story to tell. Lynn also boasts an extensive, pedestrianised shopping area and still has bustling markets held in the unusually-named Tuesday and Saturday Market Places. There are also many attractions nearby including the Norfolk coastline; much of it designated as an area of Outstanding Natural Beauty.

Places to Visit

King's Lynn Arts Centre

St George's Guildhall, 27–29 King Street, PE30 1HA
☎ 01553 764864
Live entertainment and art galleries.

King's Lynn Corn Exchange

Tuesday Market Place, PE30 1JW
☎ 01553 764864
This old building comes alive with live entertainment plus a range of other cultural activities.

Custom House

Purfleet Quay, PE30 1HP
☎ 01553 763044
Contains fascinating displays on the merchants, customs men and smugglers of Lynn.

Lynn Museum

Market Street, PE30 1NL
☎ 01553 775001
The refurbished museum holds a variety of artefacts from all ages.

The Green Quay

Marriott's Warehouse, South Quay, PE30 5DT
☎ 01553 818500
A discovery centre where you can get closer to the wildlife of the Wash.

Tales of the Old Gaol House and the Lynn Treasury

Saturday Market Place, PE30 5DQ
☎ 01553 774297
A fascinating glimpse into prison life two centuries ago, and a chance to peruse civic treasures, including the spectacular King John Cup.

Town House Museum

46 Queen Street, PE30 5DQ
☎ 01553 773450
The Town House Museum displays the social history and domestic life of Lynn's merchants, traders and families from medieval times to the 1950s.

True's Yard

North Street, PE30 1QW
☎ 01553 770479
True's Yard is all that remains of King's Lynns old fishing community, the North End.

Attractions Nearby

Castle Rising
(6 miles/9.5 km)
Castle Rising, King's Lynn,
PE31 6AH
☎ 01553 631330
One of the largest, best preserved
and most lavishly decorated keeps
in England, surrounded by twenty
acres of mighty earthworks. Take
A149 towards Hunstanton.

Houghton Hall
(14 miles/22.5km)
King's Lynn, PE31 6UE
☎ 01485 528569
Houghton Hall is a fine Palladian
mansion, set in beautiful parkland,
built in the 1720s for Sir Robert
Walpole. Seat of the Marquis
of Cholmondeley. Situated off
the A148 to Fakenham at New
Houghton.

Oxburgh Hall, Garden and Estate (NT)
(17 miles/27.5km)
Oxborough, PE33 9PS
☎ 01366 328258
Off A134 beyond Stoke Ferry on
road to Thetford. Continue visit
with Cockley Cley Iceni Village
and Museum, 3.5 miles/6km to
the northeast.
A moated manor house dated 1482
with woodland walks and trails.
Exhibits include needlework by
Mary Queen of Scots.

Sandringham House
(8 miles/12.5km)
Sandringham, PE35 6EN
☎ 01553 612908
Home of HM The Queen. Off the
A149 towards Hunstanton.

Walpole Water Gardens
(11 miles/17.5km)
Chalk Road, Walpole St. Peter,
PE14 7PH
Off A47 to Wisbech.
☎ 07718 745935

For beautiful water gardens, plants
and koi for sale all year round.
Tea room, parking facilities and
wheelchair access.

West Acre Gardens
(12 miles/19.5km)
King's Lynn, PE32 1UJ
Off A47 to Swaffham.
☎ 01760 755562
A plant lover's paradise set in an old
walled garden.

Hotels & Dining
Try the local Tourist Information
Centre, see Essential Contacts for
details.

Something Special

Hotel Elizabeth Dukes Head
Tuesday Market Place,
PE30 1JS
☎ 0870 116 2720
Georgian building in the heart of
the old town.

The Old Rectory
33 Goodwins Road, PE30 5QX
☎ 01553 768544
Elegant former rectory a short walk
through the park to the historic
centre of King's Lynn.

Bradley's Wine Bar and Restaurant
10 South Quay, PE30 5DT

☎ 01553 819888
Elegant dining on first floor of
former Georgian merchant's
home.

Rembrandt's Bistro
19 Chapel Street PE30 1EG
☎ 01553 777662
Popular eatery situated in the very
centre of King's Lynn.

Essential Contacts

Tourist Information Centre
The Custom House, Purfleet Quay,
King's Lynn, PE30 1HP
☎ 01533 763044
email: kings-lynn.tic@west-
norfolk.gov.uk
www.west-norfolk.gov.uk

Landmark Publishing gratefully
acknowledges
www.visitwestnorfolk.com
for images supplies on pages 54 & 55.

**Landmark Visitors Guide:
Norfolk & the Broads;
ISBN: 9781843063278;
£7.99**

Top – Bottom: Hill Top Farm; The World of Beatrix Potter; Holehird Gardens

Getting There

By Road

M6 from south, J36, then A590 & A591; from the north J37, A684, Kendal then A591.

By Rail & Bus

There are train companies offering a service to Windermere although you may have to change trains.

There are coach/bus companies offering a service to Windermere although you may have to make changes along the route.

Background Briefing

Beautiful Windermere is the largest natural lake in England and is a Mecca for boating enthusiasts and outdoor adventurers of all types. Walkers can enjoy glorious panoramas from the hills surrounding the lake. Watersports vary from windsurfing and kayaking to sailing and diving. Besides fell walking, land-based activities include riding, cycling, caving and climbing and if you're very brave you can even take a trip in an air balloon.

Take the footpath next to the Windermere Hotel for a walk to 'Orrest Head', an outstanding viewpoint with fine vistas over the lake. Nearby Bowness-on-Windermere is a popular tourist town delightfully situated on the lake shore. Walk along the long lakeside promenade at Bowness to enjoy wonderful views of the bustling harbour and across the lake to the mountains. The town has plenty of places to eat and drink together with many shops selling gifts, crafts, clothing and outdoor equipment. The National Park Visitor Centre at Brockhole is worth a visit. Away from the lake, visit St Martin's Church with its superb east window with some stained glass dating from the 15th century.

Ambleside is an ideal base for visiting the Lake District as it is a good starting point for many walks and excursions. Why not take the short walk which starts behind the Salutation Hotel to Stock Ghyll Force, a spectacular 70ft waterfall, or stroll around the 'Ambleside Heritage Trail' which takes you through the old town and its interesting buildings. This busy town is also packed with cafes, restaurants and specialist shops. Troutbeck is a pretty village with a number of buildings which date from the 17th to the 19th centuries. Waterhead at the north end of Windermere is a picturesque stop for the cruisers, with cafes and a garden centre. Lakeside, at the southern end, has the terminus of the Lakeside and Haverthwaite Railway.

Places to Visit

Rydal Mount & Gardens

Rydal, near Ambleside, LA22 9LU
☎ 015394 33002
www.rydalmount.co.uk

The home of the Wordsworth family for forty-six years until the death of Mary Wordsworth in 1859. Rydal Mount was the largest house the Wordsworths lived in and became a much-loved family home. The garden has hardly changed since Wordsworth's day.

The National Park Visitor Centre (Brockhole)

Windermere, LA23 1LJ
☎ 015394 46601
www.visitcumbria.com

A Victorian house set in thirty acres of magnificent terraced gardens stretching down to the shore of Windermere. There are interactive exhibitions and audiovisual information, a shop and a restaurant. In the grounds are a picnic area and an adventure playground and you can take a cruise from the lakeshore.

Other Places to Visit

Abbot Hall Art Gallery

Kendal, LA9 5AL
☎ 01539 722464
www.abbothall.org.uk

Aquarium of the Lakes

Lakeside, Newby Bridge, LA12 8AS
☎ 015395 30153
www.aquariumofthelakes.co.uk

Blackwell – Arts & Crafts House

Bowness-on-Windermere, LA23 3JT
☎ 015394 46139

A fine arts and crafts house, open as a gallery for craft and applied art.

Holehird Gardens

The Lakeland Horticultural Society, Patterdale Road, Windermere LA23 1NP
☎ 015394 46008
www.holehirdgardens.org.uk

Lakeside & Haverthwaite Railway

Haverthwaite Station, Ulverston,

Lake Windermere

LA12 8AL
☎ 015395 31594
www.lakesiderailway.co.uk
Steam trains running a seasonal daily service from Haverthwaite to Lakeside via the Leven valley.

The World of Beatrix Potter Attraction
The Old Laundry, Crag Brow, Bowness-on-Windermere, LA23 3BX
☎ 015394 88444
www.hop-skip-jump.com

Attractions Nearby

Levens Hall and Gardens
(13 miles/21.5km)
Levens, Kendal, LA8 0PD
☎ 015395 60321
www.levenshall.co.uk
Elizabethan mansion with world famous topiary garden.

Museum of Lakeland Life
(8.5 miles/13.5km)
Abbot Hall, Kendal, LA9 5AL
☎ 01539 722464
This award-winning museum takes you back through time to tell the story of the Lake District and its inhabitants.

Townend (NT)
(2.5 miles/4km)
Troutbeck, LA23 1LB
☎ 015394 32628
17th century Lake District stone and slate house, former home of a wealthy farming family.

Sizergh Castle & Garden (NT)
(11 miles/17.5km)
Sizergh, Kendal, LA8 8AE
☎ 015395 60951

Medieval house with Tudor additions surrounded by a superb garden and large estate.

Events

The Bowness Theatre Festival

Kirkland Festival

Lake District Summer Music Festival

Windermere on Water (WOW) Festival

Hotels & Dining
Try the local Tourist Information Centre, see Essentail Contacts for details.
The Lake District has many fine-country house hotels to choose from and lots of in-town accommodation.

Something Special

Gilpin Lodge Country House Hotel
Crook Road, Windermere, LA23 3NE
☎ 015394 88818
www.gilpinlodge.co.uk
A luxury country house hotel set in twenty acres in the Lake District National Park. Gilpin Lodge has earned many awards and accolades for both accommodation and dining. An added bonus is the availability of on-call therapists who provide spa treatments in your room.

Holbeck Ghyll Country House Hotel
Holbeck Lane, Windermere, LA23 1LU
☎ 015394 32375
www.holbeckghyll.com
Majestically situated overlooking Lake Windermere with a Michelin Star restaurant and a wonderful health spa.

Jerichos Restaurant
At the Waverley Hotel, College Road, Windermere, LA23 1BX
☎ 015394 42522
Award-winning restaurant described as 'a true culinary gem'.

The Hideaway at Windermere
Phoenix Way, Windermere, LA23 1DB
☎ 015394 43070
www.thehideawayatwindermere.co.uk
Fine restaurant open to non-residents serving British food with a creative twist.

Rothay Manor House Hotel and Restaurant
Ambleside, Cumbria, LA22 0EH
☎ 015394 33605
Dine in this elegant Regency country house hotel with a restaurant widely acclaimed for its culinary expertise.

Landmark Trust
Howthwaite, Grasmere
Immediately behind Wordsworth's Dove Cottage, sleeps seven.

Essential Contacts

Tourist Information Centres
Victoria Street, Windermere, LA23 1AD
☎ 015394 4649

Glebe Road, Bowness-on-Windermere, LA23 3HJ
☎ 015394 42895

Central Buildings, Market Cross, Ambleside, LA22 9BT
☎ 015394 32582

Windermere Lake Cruises
The Promenade, Bowness-on-Windermere, LA23 3HQ
☎ 015394 43360
www.windermere-lakecruises.co.uk

Left: Lincoln Cathedral in the historic city of Lincoln; Right Top – Bottom: The Lincoln Crown Court is located within the Lincoln castle grounds; Lincoln has many historic buildings; View from Lincoln Walls

Getting There

By Road

From the south – A1 to Newark, then north on the A46.

From the north – A1 to Markham Moor then on the A57.

By Rail & Bus

There is a rail service into Lincoln station from around the country although you may have to make changes to complete the journey.

Most coach/bus operators offer a service to Lincoln.

Background Briefing

Step back in time in this fascinating city with an impressive architectural heritage. Discover Roman gates, a Norman castle, a medieval square and the magnificent Romanesque and Gothic cathedral. Minster Yard has a number of fine Georgian and medieval houses, and close by are the ruins of the medieval Bishop's Palace. Head down Steep Hill, a cobbled lane lined with interesting and unusual specialist shops, into the High Street Quarter where you will find several shopping centres. You can enjoy a show at the Drill Hall or a play at the Edwardian Theatre Royal in the Cultural Quarter. Stroll along the Brayford Waterfront where there is a multiplex cinema and many places to eat and drink as well as the opportunity to watch colourful narrow boats and pleasure craft or indulge in a relaxing boat trip.

Lincoln can easily be explored on foot so why not book a walking tour or a ghost walk, or alternatively visit the sights on Lincoln's Walk and Ride service which allows you to hop on and off at thirteen stops around the city centre. Look out for the 12th century Jew's House, the Stonebow and Guildhall, visit art galleries and museums and enjoy street theatre, buskers and markets in this vibrant cosmopolitan city. Farmers' Markets are held three times a month in various locations. The popular Christmas Market is reputedly the second largest in the world when Lincoln is filled with festive spirit, having stalls and attractions spread throughout the city.

Peace and tranquillity can be found in the heart of the city at The Lawn where you will find a tropical conservatory and the John Dawber Garden. After a successful shopping spree, stroll to the Arboretum, a fine Victorian park with a bandstand and a perfect place for a picnic. Don't miss The Collection, a fabulous new Museum embracing The Usher, the region's premier art gallery.

Places to Visit

Bishop's Palace
Minster Yard, LN2 1PU
☎ 01522 527468
Once one of the most important buildings in the country, reflecting the power and wealth of the Prince Bishops. See the impressive barrel vaulted, undercrofted 12th century Great Hall, chapel range and the entrance tower, the vineyard and the heritage garden. The award-winning audio tour is recommended.

Lincoln Cathedral
Minster Yard, LN2 1PZ
☎ 01522 544544
www.lincolncathedral.com
This stunning gothic cathedral, with its soaring towers, dominates the skyline and is one of the finest medieval buildings in Europe. The splendid West Front with its Romanesque frieze, St Hugh's choir with its tierceron vault and carved choir stalls, the Chapter House and the magnificent nave with Victorian stained glass windows will delight the discerning visitor. Don't miss the Dean's Eye rose window in the North Transept which is one of the most important examples of medieval stained glass in Europe and don't forget to look for the Lincoln Imp. Recently the Cathedral was

used as a film set for the 'Da Vinci Code' blockbuster.

Lincoln Castle
Castle Hill, LN1 3AA
☎ 01522 511068
This impressive Norman castle stands on a site occupied since Roman times. Today you can see the prison chapel, dungeons and one of only four surviving copies of the Magna Carta. Tour the towers and walk the castle walls for stunning views across the city. In summer months open-air concerts and al fresco performances are held in the castle grounds.

The Collection
Danes Terrace, LN2 1 LP
☎ 01522 550990
Exciting new museum with a wealth of artefacts from the Stone, Bronze and Iron Ages, Roman, Saxon, Viking and Medieval eras. The Collection includes fine, decorative and contemporary visual arts and temporary exhibitions. Situated next to the Usher Gallery, the region's largest contemporary and traditional arts venue.

Lincoln Arboretum
Monks Road, LN5 7AY
☎ 01522 873423

Museum of Lincolnshire Life
Burton Road, LN1 3LY
☎ 01522 528448
Social history museum next to a working 18th century windmill.

Attractions Nearby

The Dambusters Heritage Centre
(6 miles/9.5km)
Scampton Village
☎ 01522 731333
A large photographic collection relating to the famous dams raid and RAF Scampton in 1943.

Top - Bottom: Castle at dusk; Brayford Pool; Lincoln Glory Hole; Cathedral interior; Steep Hill

Lincoln Castle

Doddington Hall
(7.5 miles/12km)
Doddington, LN6 4RU
☎ 01522 694 308
A magnificent Elizabethan mansion.

Woodside Falconry and Conservation Centre
(8.5 miles/13.5km)
Newball, Near Langworth, LN3 5DQ
☎ 01522 754280
www.woodsidefalconry.com
A fun day out for all the family.

Rand Farm Park
(10.5 miles/17km)
Rand LN8 5NJ
☎ 01673 858904
Feed, touch and hold animals at this working farm.

Events

Brayford Waterfront Festival

Lincoln Book Festival

Lincoln Christmas Market

Chamber Music Festival

Lincoln Early Music Festival

Lincoln Jazz Festival

Lincolnshire Sausage Festival

Hotels & Dining

Try the local Tourist Information Centre, see Essential Contacts for details.

Something Special

The White Hart Hotel
Bailgate, LN1 3AR
☎ 01522 526 222
www.whitehart-lincoln.co.uk
In a prime position near to cathedral and castle with luxurious rooms and delicious dining in the Grille Restaurant.

Washingborough Hall Hotel
Church Hill, Washingborough, LN4 1BE
☎ 01522 790340
www.washingboroughhall.com
A beautiful Georgian manor house situated in four acres of landscaped gardens and just two miles from the centre of Lincoln. The Wedgwood Restaurant's modern European menu is based on local produce and includes Lincolnshire sausages and cheeses complimented by a carefully selected wine list.

Branston Hall Hotel
Branston, LN4 1PD
☎ 01522 793305
An elegant country house set in eighty-eight acres of wooded parkland and lakes, just three miles from Lincoln. The hotel has a swimming pool together with Simpsons Spa therapy and beauty treatments.

Landmark Trust
The Chateau, Gate Burton, around fourteen miles northwest from Lincoln, sleeps three.

Why Not?
2 Brayford Quays, LN1 1YW
☎ 01522 521112
www.whynotlincoln.co.uk
Sophisticated cocktail lounge and restaurant with Black Rock Grill.

Castlegate Restaurant
Union Road, LN1 3BJ
☎ 01522 520883
www.castlegaterestaurant.com
Fine dining in the Cathedral Quarter.

Essential Contacts

Tourist Information Centres
9 Castle Hill, Cathedral Quarter
LN1 3AA
☎ 01522 873213

21 The Cornhill, High Street, LN5 7HB
☎ 01522 873256

Lincoln Boat trips
Lucy Tower Street, Brayford Pool, next to the Harbourmasters Office
☎ 01522 881200
www.lincolnboattrips.com

Cathedral City Cruises
☎ 01522 546853

City of Lincoln Guided Tours
9 Castle Hill, LN1 3AA
☎ 01522 873213

Drill Hall
Freeschool Lane, LN2 1EY
☎ 01522873894

Theatre Royal
Clasketgate, Lincoln, LN2 1JJ
☎ 01522 534570
www.theatreroyallincoln.com

Landmark Publishing gratefully acknowledges Lincolnshire Tourism for the images supplied on pages 59 & 60.
www.visitlincolnshire.com

Liverpool, Merseyside

Pier Head buildings from across the River Mersey

Getting There

By Road

Liverpool is well serviced by the motorway network.

By Rail & Bus

There are train services into Liverpool from around the country.

The main coach/bus operators call at Liverpool bus stations.

You may need to make changes to complete your journey.

Background Briefing

Liverpool, the European Capital of Culture 2008, certainly lives up to the name, having more galleries, museums and theatres than any other city outside London. Culture vultures, shopaholics and sporting enthusiasts will not be disappointed by this exciting, passionate city. Liverpool is a shopper's paradise where there are many shopping areas including the Met Quarter, Cavern Walks, St John's and the new Liverpool 1. Several Farmers' Markets are held at weekends every month throughout the city.

Liverpool, still a working port, has a unique maritime history and its historic waterfront is now a Unesco World Heritage Site. A walk from the Pier Head past the Three Graces (the Cunard Building, the Port of Liverpool Building and of course the Royal Liver Building with its famous liver birds) will lead to the Albert Dock and many interesting attractions. Tate Liverpool, housed in an impressive converted warehouse, has the largest collections of modern and contemporary art outside London. The docks also have the Maritime Museum and the Custom and Excise Museum.

The city is well known as the birthplace of the Beatles and The Beatles Story, on the Albert Dock, takes the visitor on a journey into the life, times, culture and music of the four lads from Liverpool. Intrepid visitors could take a Duck Tour (DWCK), in an authentic World War II landing vehicle, touring the waterfront before splashing into the Salthouse Dock. For the less adventurous a leisurely river cruise is ideal and the nostalgic appeal of a ferry across the Mersey cannot be ignored. Why not combine a trip on the ferry with a visit to Spaceport based at Seacombe Ferry Terminal.

Away from the dock area are many architectural gems including the magnificent 18th century Town Hall, the Princes Road Synagogue, the Victorian glasshouse at Sefton Park, the neo-classical St George's Hall, two cathedrals and the 15th century Speke Hall.

Depending on the time of year sports fans have a choice of race-courses, golf and international tennis tournaments and football clubs. Keen supporters can enjoy a club museum and stadium tour at Anfield. To appreciate all that this lively city has to offer book a walking tour or take one of the sightseeing tour buses. Venture into the surrounding area and take a trip on a tram at Birkenhead, visit the Wirral peninsula, Southport's classic promenade pier and beaches, or the beach statues at Crosby.

Places to Visit

Beatles Story

Britannia Vaults, Albert Dock, L3 4AD
☎ 0151 7091963
www.beatlesstory.com

Liverpool Cathedral

St James Mount L1 7AZ
☎ 0151 709 6271
The largest cathedral in the UK, with the world's highest Gothic arches, Sir John Betjeman called it "one of the great buildings of the twentieth century". Panoramic views from the tower, the Elizabeth Hoare Embroidery Gallery and now boasting a new attraction – the Great Space.

Mendips & 20 Forthlin Road (NT)

There is no direct access by car or on foot to Mendips; visits are by combined minibus tour only with 20 Forthlin Road.
20 Forthlin Road, Allerton, L24 1YP
☎ 0844 800 4791
Mendips, where John Lennon lived with his Aunt Mimi, was bought by Yoko Ono Lennon and immediately donated to the National

Top – Bottom: Liver Building and globe; Liverpool has many imposing buildings; Majestic Lime Street Hotel

Trust, who opened the house to the public. 20 Forthlin Road is the childhood home of Paul McCartney.

Merseyside Maritime Museum
Albert Dock, L3 4AQ
☎ 0151 478 4499
www.liverpoolmuseums.org.uk
Four floors of fascinating galleries that explore the city's maritime legacy. Discover Liverpool's important role during World War II, life at sea with the merchant navy and

the brand new Titanic, Lusitania and Forgotten Empress gallery.

Tate Liverpool
Albert Dock, L3 4BB
☎ 0151 702 7400
www.tate.org.uk
Selected works from the Tate Collection and special exhibitions of artwork from around the world.

Underwater Street
Cunard Building, Water Street, L3 1DS
☎ 0151 227 2550
www.underwaterstreet.com
A unique hands-on discovery centre for families of children aged up to ten. Lots of painting and creative activities plus a cafe.

Beatles Magical Mystery Tour
☎ 0151 2369091
www.cavernclub.org
Tour places associated with the Beatles on board a vintage bus.

Customs & Excise National Museum
Albert Dock, L3 4AQ
☎ 0151 478 4499
Discover the exciting and intriguing story of smuggling and contraband.

Mr Hardman's Home Photographic Studio (NT)
59 Rodney Street, L1 9EX
☎ 0151 709 6261
Georgian house and former home of Liverpool photographer Edward Chambré Hardman.

Liverpool Football Club Museum and Stadium Tour
Anfield
☎ 0151 260 6677
www.liverpoolfc.tv

Walker Art Gallery
William Brown Street, L3 8EL
☎ 0151 478 4199
www.liverpoolmuseums.org.uk
One of the finest art galleries in Europe with art from medieval times to the 21st century.

National Wildflower Centre
Court Hey Park, Roby Road L16 3NA
☎ 0151 738 1913
www.wildflower.co.uk
Set in a tranquil Victorian park, the National Wildflower Centre is a beautiful visitor attraction with a difference.

Attractions Nearby

Speke Hall (NT)
(8 miles/13km)
The Walk, L24 1XD
☎ 0151 427 7231
The finest surviving timber framed Tudor manor house in the northwest of England. Enjoy beautiful country walks with stunning views.

Sunlight Vision Museum
(6 miles/10km)
23 King George's Drive, Port Sunlight, CH62 5DX
☎ 0151 644 6466
A good place to begin a visit to this amazing village. Portrays the way of

Left: Liverpool skyline in the area of the Pier Head; Right: The promenade, Albert Dock

life for the very first villagers and workers of Port Sunlight during late Victorian and Edwardian times.

The Lady Lever Art Gallery
(6 miles/10km)
Port Sunlight Village,
CH62 5EQ
☎ 0151 478 4136
www.liverpoolmuseums.org.uk
One of the most beautiful collections of fine and decorative arts in the country.

Spaceport
(5.5 miles/9km)
Victoria Place, Seacombe,
Wallasey, CH44 6QY
☎ 0151 330 1333
www.spaceport.org.uk
Take a virtual journey through space.

Wirral Museum
(3 miles/5km)
Hamilton Square, Birkenhead,
CH41 5BR
☎ 0151 666 4010
www.visitliverpool.com
Displays include the history of Cammell Laird, tracing the shipbuilder's rise and fall.

Events
Africa Oye
Brouhaha International Street Festival
Dadafest
Fiesta Latina
The Grand National, Aintree
Homotopia
Honda F4 Powerboat Liverpool Grand Prix
Hope Street Festival
Comedy Festival
International Tennis Tournament

Irish Festival
Music Week
Mathew Street Music Festival
Summer Pops
The Open Golf Championship
Writing on the Wall Festival

Hotels & Dining
Try the Tourist Information Centre accommodation booking services.
☎ 0844 870 0123
email: bookaroom@merseyside.org.uk

Something Special

Hope Street Hotel
40 Hope Street, L1 9DA
☎ 0151 7093000
www.hopestreethotel.co.uk
A fabulous boutique hotel in the city centre.

Radisson SAS Hotel Liverpool
107 Old Hall Street, L3 9BD
☎ 0151 9661500
www.radisson.com
Conveniently located near the waterfront with an award-winning restaurant offering modern Italian cuisine. Ark Health and Fitness Club.

Alma de Cuba
St Peter's Church, Seel Street,
L1 4BH
☎ 0151 7027394
www.alma-de-cuba.com
Set in a magnificently converted former Catholic church.

Blue Bar and Grill
Albert Dock, L3 0AJ
☎ 0151 7025831
www.blue-venue.co.uk
Stylish restaurant in a unique setting, offering an interesting variety of dishes.

Essential Contacts
Albert Dock Visitor Information Centre
Anchor Courtyard, Albert Dock,
L3 4BS

City Centre TIC
08 Place, 36–38 Whitechapel,
L1 6DZ
☎ 0151 2332008
www.visitliverpool.com

City Sightseeing
☎ 0151 2033920
Hop-on hop-off open top bus.

Echo Arena
Monarchs Quay, L3 4FP
(Sat nav L3 4BX)
☎ 0844 8000 400
www.accliverpool.com
Lively entertainment centre.

Empire Theatre
Lime Street, L1 1JE
☎ 0870 606 3536
www.liverpoolempire.org.uk

Everyman Theatre
13 Hope Street, L1 9BH
☎ 0151 709 4776

Liverpool Playhouse
Williamson Square, L1 1EL
☎ 0151 709 4776

Mersey Ferries
Victoria Place, Seacombe,
CH44 6QY
☎ 0151 330 1444

Duck Tours
Anchor Courtyard, Albert Dock,
L3 4AS
☎ 0151 708 7799
www.theyellowduckmarine.co.uk

Philharmonic Hall
Hope Street, L1 9BP
☎ 0151 709 3789

Royal Court Theatre
Roe Street, L1 1HL
☎ 0870 787 1866

Dinham medieval bridge on the River Teme and Ludlow

Getting There

By Road

On the A49, Leominster – Shrewsbury road.

By Train & Bus

Ludlow station, on the Marches line. Good connections at Crewe, Shrewsbury and Newport (South Wales).

There are no direct coach routes to Ludlow; check online for local bus routes from Shrewsbury.

Background Briefing

Ludlow, a medieval market town in the Welsh Marches, resonates with history at every corner. The streets are lined with wonderful medieval and Georgian buildings. Indeed Ludlow has over 500 listed buildings including the half-timbered Feathers Hotel. The hotel, originally built as a merchant's house in 1619, acquired its name because of the motifs of ostrich feathers forming part of the timber facade. Broad Street, often described as the most beautiful street in Britain, has the 18th century Buttercross at the top and the Broadgate at the bottom. Ludlow's compact centre is easy to explore on foot and a gentle stroll will take the visitor past fascinating period architecture, a magnificent church and the ruins of a fine medieval castle. There are special 'Walking for Life' waymarkers around the town and the Ludlow Historical Research Group lead guided walks

during the summer.

Ghost walks also take place every Friday at 8pm starting at the Buttercross, outside the Church Inn (seasonal only). St Laurence's Church is one of the largest in England, reflecting the prosperity of the wool trade in the town in the Middle Ages. The church, largely rebuilt in the 15th century in a soaring perpendicular style, has features of the Norman, Early English and Decorated periods. It has a glorious vaulted ceiling and contains fine misericords and bench ends. The poet A.E. Housman, author of '*A Shropshire Lad*', is commemorated in the churchyard.

Long regarded as the gastronomic capital of Shropshire, Ludlow has deservedly acquired a reputation for being the centre for some of the best food and drink in Britain. Ludlow is a shopper's paradise with a fantastic range of independent shops, weekly markets and a twice-monthly farmers' market. With over 500 listed buildings, mainly Georgian or half-timbered, Ludlow is an architectural treat.

Ludlow Festival is held in June/July, attracting performers from all over the world. A food and drink festival takes place in September and in November the Medieval Christmas Fair is held locally. Rowing boats can be hired on the river below the castle and expeditions undertaken to the beautiful countryside surrounding the town.

Places to Visit

Ludlow Castle

Castle Square, SY8 1AY
www.ludlowcastle.com
The finest of medieval ruined castles, set in glorious Shropshire countryside, at the heart of this superb, bustling black and white market town.

Ludlow Museum

Castle Square, SY8 1AS
☎ 01584 813666
www.shropshire.gov.uk
The museum tells the story of the people who have lived and worked in Ludlow, from Bronze Age farmers through to the present day. Also has a geology gallery.

Linney Riverside Park

On fields below Ludlow Castle. Relax in a peaceful setting beside the River Teme. Rowing boats for hire Easter–September, with putting green and picnic area.

Attractions Nearby

Angel Gardens

(4 miles/7km)
Springfield Angel Lane, SY8 3HZ
☎ 01584 890381
Angel Gardens are beautiful ornamental gardens located in an Area of Outstanding Natural Beauty near

All above: Stokesay Castle

Ludlow. Situated at 1000 feet above sea level they have panoramic views of the stunning Shropshire countryside and Welsh ranges.

Ludlow Racecourse
Bromfield, SY8 2BT
☎ 01584 856221
www.ludlowracecourse.co.uk
Just north of Ludlow off the A49.

Stokesay Castle (EH)
(7 miles/12km)
Craven Arms, SY7 9AH
☎ 01588 672544
Stokesay Castle is the finest and best preserved 13th century fortified manor house in England. Take the A49 towards Shrewsbury. (Shropshire Hills Discovery Centre is a short distance beyond here.)

Shropshire Hills Discovery Centre
(7 miles/12km)
School Road, Craven Arms SY7 9RS
☎ 01588 676000
A range of activities, pasttimes and opportunities for everyone and anyone.

Berrington Hall (NT)
(8 miles/14km)
nr Leominster, HR6 0DW
☎ 01568 615721
Neo-classical mansion with fine interiors, set in landscaped grounds.

Land of Lost Content
(8 miles/14 km)
The Market Hall, Market Street, Craven Arms, SY7 9NW
☎ 01588 676176
National Museum of British Popular Culture.

Events

September 12–14th Food & Drink Festival
www.foodfestival.co.uk
For details of the Country Fair, Craft Fair, Local Produce Markets and Flea Markets.

Above & Left: Ludlow town centre

Above Right: View from inside the Market Hall

www.visitludlow.co.uk

Hotels & Dining
Try the local Tourist Information Centre, see Essential Contacts.

Something Special

De Grey's
Broad Street, SY8 1BG
☎ 01584 872764
www.degreys.co.uk
Five star accommodation in an Elizabethan townhouse.

Fishmore Hall
Fishmore Road, SY8 3DP
www.fishmorehall.co.uk
☎ 01584 875148
A beautifully restored Regency house on a hill overlooking the town.

Landmark Trust
Broomfield Priory Gatehouse, nr Ludlow
Built pre-1400, with first floor added after the Dissolution. Sleeps six.

La Bécasse
17 Corve Street, SY8 1DA
☎ 01584 872325
www.labecasse.co.uk
Modern French cuisine.

Mr Underhill's
Dinham Weir, SY8 1EH
☎ 01584 874431
www.mr-underhills.co.uk
Michelin starred restaurant in stunning setting beside the river with accommodation.

Essential Contacts

Ludlow Visitor Information
Castle Street, SY8 1AS
☎ 01584 875053

Ghost Walks
Every Friday.
www.shropshireghostwalks.co.uk

Ludlow Assembly Rooms
Mill Street, SY8 1AZ
☎ 01584 878141
www.ludlowassemblyrooms.co.uk
Lively arts and community centre.

Getting There

By Road

North: M5 at J28/A373 to Hointon/A35/A3052.
South: M5 J29/A30 to Hointon/A35/A3052.

By Train & Bus

The London Waterloo–Exeter service stops at Axminster, then take the number 31 bus for the final twenty minute journey to Lyme Regis.

Background Briefing

Charming, genteel Lyme Regis, with its steep narrow lanes and

Top – Bottom: The harbour, Lyme Regis; Barrington Court; Beer; Deck chairs on the seafront

lovely Georgian, Regency and Victorian houses, is an unspoilt seaside resort and fishing port. The town, on the edge of the Jurassic Coast, is popular with fossil hunters and is famous as the place where a complete ichthyosaurus skeleton was discovered in 1811. Even today giant ammonite fossils can be seen in pavements and walls. Lyme is best appreciated on foot so that its narrow lanes and streets can be properly explored; walk along the famous Cobb, immortalised in the film of John Fowles' novel, *The French Lieutenant's Woman*, where there are ample places to rest and appreciate the fine views out to sea or watch the activities of fishing boats and pleasure craft. Lyme Regis has been welcoming visitors since the 18th century and Jane Austen stayed here when writing *Persuasion*, which is partly set in Lyme.

Today the town has safe, sheltered south-facing beaches and a traffic-free promenade where children can safely play. Langmoor and Lister Gardens and the Jane Austen Garden provide welcome areas to stroll or sit in superb settings and enjoy wonderful views. The Undercliff National Nature Reserve, to the west of the town, is only accessible to walkers and is a lovely unspoilt area of the coast where many species of wild flowers can be found. More adventurous walkers will appreciate the Heritage Coast footpath which stretches for twenty miles to the east and west of Lyme.

Activities abound in Lyme and you can go on a fossil walk, take a scenic boat trip, go sailing, deep sea fishing or catch mackerel and crabs. The more energetic can swim, windsurf, body board or dive. There is a traditional seaside theatre, a cinema, art galleries and museums.

Shoppers will enjoy the numerous souvenir, fossil and craft shops and the tea rooms and cafes throughout the town. Lyme Regis is known as the Pearl of Dorset and is set amid breathtaking scenery, making it an ideal base for visits to picturesque villages and the beautiful surrounding countryside.

Places to Visit

Lyme Regis Museum

Bridge Street DT7 3QA
☎ 01297 443370
www.lymeregismuseum.co.uk
The Philpot Museum is housed in a magnificent, historic building and is packed with exhibits in a series of galleries.

The Town Mill

Mill Lane, DT7 3PU
☎ 01297 443579
www.townmill.org.uk
A restored working water mill dating from 1340 with two art galleries, an arts and crafts studio, pottery, frame-maker, restaurant and 17th century walled garden. The Town Mill path, an attractive woodland walk, links the town via Broad Street car park with the Town Mill and historic Coombe Street.

Dinosaurland

Coombe Street, DT7 3PY
☎ 01297 443541
A fossil museum with an extensive display of local Jurassic marine fossils.

Lyme Regis Marine Aquarium

The Cobb
☎ 01297 444230
www.lymeregismarineaquarium.co.uk

Attractions Nearby

Barrington Court (NT)

(22 miles/36km)

Barrington, nr Ilminster,
TA19 0NQ
☎ 01460 242614
Large beautiful Jekyll-inspired gardens. Tudor manor, let to Stuart Interiors and used as showrooms for antique and reproduction furniture.

Abbotsbury Sub Tropical Gardens
(18 miles/29km)
Abbotsbury, Weymouth,
DT3 4LA
☎ 01305 871817
www.abbotsbury-tourism.co.uk
Magnificent Victorian walled garden set in twenty acres of woodland valley, filled with rare and exotic plants from all over the world.

Abbotsbury Swannery
(21 miles/33km)
New Barn Road, Abbotsbury,
nr Weymouth, DT3 4JG
☎ 01305 87185
A unique location where it is possible to walk through the heart of a colony of nesting mute swans.

Charmouth Heritage Coast Centre
(3 miles/5km)
Lower Sea Lane, Charmouth,
DT6 6LL
☎ 01297 560772
www.charmouth.org

Seaton Tramway
(7.5 miles/12km)
Riverside Depot, Harbour Road,
Seaton EX12 2NQ
☎ 01297 20375
www.tram.co.uk

Forde Abbey and Gardens
(13 miles/21km)
Chard, TA20 4LU
☎ 01460 221290
www.fordeabbey.co.uk
An elegant former Cistercian monastery with thirty acres of exquisite award-winning gardens.

Events
Lyme Regis Jazz Festival
Lyme Regis Lifeboat Week
Lyme Regis Regatta & Carnival Week
Lyme Regis ArtsFest

Hotels & Dining
Accommodation can be booked through the local Tourist Information Centre, see Essential Contacts for details.

Something Special

Alexandra Hotel and Restaurant
Pound Street, Lyme Regis,
DT7 3HZ
☎ 01297 442010
email: enquiries@hotelalexandra.co.uk
www.hotelalexandra.co.uk

The Orchard Country Hotel
Rousdon, Lyme Regis
DT7 3XW
☎ 01297 442972
www.orchardcountryhotel.com
Just three miles from Lyme Regis.

Landmark Trust
Margells, Branscombe
A lovely cottage dating from the end of the 16th Century. Sleeps five. The nearby pub is described by the Trust as being 'distinctly agreeable'!

The Broad Street Restaurant
58 Broad Street, DT7 3QF
☎ 01297 445792
A lovely restaurant in one of the town's most historic buildings, with an excellent menu using fresh produce from local sources including meat and fish.

The Riverside Restaurant
West Bay, Bridport, DT6 4EZ

Top: The Cobb; **Bottom:** Beautiful thatched cottage

☎ 01308 422011
www.thefishrestaurant-westbay.co.uk

Essential Contacts

The Lyme Regis Tourist Information Centre
Guildhall Cottage, Church Street,
DT7 3BS
☎ 01297 442138
email: lymeregis.tic@westdorset-dc.gov.uk

Boat Trips
☎ 07890 739625
www.lymebayboattrips.co.uk

Fossil Walks
☎ 01297 443370

Guided Fossil Walks with Dr Colin Dawes
The Old Forge Fossil Shop, 15 Broad Street, Lyme Regis, DT7 3QE
☎ 01297 443758

Fossil Hunting Trips
☎ 07944 664 757
www.lymeregisfossilwalks.com

Marine Theatre
Church Street, DT7 3Q
☎ 01297 442138
www.marinetheatre.com

Landmark Visitors Guide: Dorset;
ISBN: 9781843063117;
£9.99

Manchester

Salford Quays at dusk

Getting There

By Road

Manchester is well served by the road network, with motorways leading into the city from all points.

By Rail & Bus

There are rail services into Manchester stations from around the country.

Most of the main coach/bus operators offer a service to Manchester although you may need to change to complete the journey.

Background Briefing

Manchester is a lively, cosmopolitan city with a wide range of attractions to visit by day together with a buzzing nightlife. The city boasts one of the best live music scenes anywhere and has entertainment venues offering dancing, music, comedy, ballet, opera and musical theatre. The shopping is fantastic and will suit every taste from exclusive designer shoppers to bargain hunters. There are speciality shops throughout Manchester while larger centres include the Triangle shopping centre and the Arndale Centre, or head outside the city to the Trafford Centre, the largest in the UK. There are regular weekly markets and a twice-monthly Farmers' and Produce Market at Piccadilly Gardens on Fridays and Saturdays. Restaurants, cafes and bars cater for every taste; the range on offer enables you to sample cuisine from around the world. You will find chic cafe bars under the renovated railway arches at Deansgate Locks and spectacular views over the city from a comfortable capsule on the observation wheel in Exchange Square.

Manchester's architecture is imposing and grand with many Victorian and Edwardian buildings, from the impressive Gothic Revival Town Hall, completed in 1887, to the elaborate Opera House on Quay Street, built in 1912 and the contemporary Midland Hotel. Don't miss Charles Barry's elegant Greek building on Mosley Street, now the Manchester Art Gallery, begun in 1825 for the Royal Institution. Museums, art galleries and libraries galore invite the visitor to enter their portals and sample their respective treasures. For stunning modern architecture see 'Urbis' in Cathedral Gardens and then step inside to take a ride through different cities around the world and experience interactive exhibits and dynamic changing exhibitions.

When it's time for some rest and relaxation head for the public open space in Cathedral Gardens or visit the beautiful, Bulie Park in Salford with eighty-seven acres of national and historic importance. No visit to Manchester is complete without a trip to Salford Quays, just fifteen minutes by tram from the city centre, where you will find The Lowry, the Imperial War Museum North, the Manchester United Museum and Tour and the Lowry Outlet Mall. There's a water sports centre where the more adventurous visitors can try their hand at rowing, sailing, canoeing and windsurfing. One of the best ways to see all that the city offers is to take a Hop-On Hop-Off Bus Tour from St Peter's Square, or enquire at the visitor centre about the many themed guided walks. Around Manchester are a variety of stately homes and gardens, interesting industrial heritage and the stunning country of Lancashire and the Peak District.

Places to Visit

Imperial War Museum North
Trafford Wharf Road, The Quays, M17 1TZ
☎ 0161 836 4000
www.iwm.org.uk/north/
Thought-provoking museum, in an award-winning building, using projected images and sound to tell the story of how war and conflict have shaped people's lives.

The Lowry
Pier Eight, Salford Quays
M50 3AZ
☎ 0161 876 2000
www.thelowry.com
Art gallery, theatres, restaurants and much more.

Urbis
Cathedral Gardens, M4 3BG
☎ 0161 605 8200
www.urbis.org.uk
Take a ride through different cities of the world at this fascinating exhibition centre featuring interactive displays, and discover a 3D satellite view of any city on the planet.

Greater Manchester Police Museum
Newton Street, M1 2ES
☎ 0161 856 3287
www.gmp.police.uk

Manchester Art Gallery
Mosley Street, M2 3JL
☎ 0161 235 8888
www.manchestergalleries.org

Manchester City Experience Tour
City of Manchester Stadium, Sportcity Eastlands, M11 3FF
☎ 0870 062 1894
www.mcfc.co.uk

Manchester United Museum and Tour
Sir Matt Busby Way, Old Trafford, M16 0RA
☎ 0870 442 1994
www.manutd.com
Re-live the club's triumphs, tragedies and trophies at this museum with a difference, and delve behind the scenes at the Theatre of Dreams by taking the Stadium Tour.

Whitworth Art Gallery
Oxford Road, M15 6ER
☎ 0161 275 7450
www.manchester.ac.uk

The Museum of Science & Industry
Liverpool Road, Castlefield, M3 4FP
☎ 0161 832 2244
www.mosi.org.uk

Attractions Nearby

Quarry Bank Mill
(11 miles/17.5km)
Styal Estate, Wilmslow, SK9 4LA
☎ 01625 527 468
www.quarrybankmill.org.uk
An 18th century water powered cotton mill with working machinery set in a beautiful (NT) country park. Don't miss the restored Apprentice House and the mill owner's private garden.

Bramall Hall
(10 miles/16km)
Bramhall Park, Bramhall
SK7 3NX
☎ 0161 485 3708
www.stockport.gov.uk
A superb example of a Cheshire 14th century black and white timber-framed manor house set in beautiful parkland.

Dunham Massey Hall (NT)
(11 miles/18km)
Dunham Massey, Altrincham, WA14 4SJ
☎ 0161 941 1025
A complete country estate with a house, garden and deer park at its centre.

East Lancashire Railway
(9 miles/14.5km)
Bolton Street Station, Bury, BL9 0EY
☎ 0161 764 7790
www.east-lancs-rly.co.uk
A beautifully restored steam railway running along the Irwell Valley.

Hatworks
(7.5 miles/12km)
Wellington Mill, Wellington Road South, Stockport, SK3 0EU
☎ 0161 355 7770
www.hatworks.org.uk
The UK's only museum dedicated to hats and the hatting industry.

River Irwel, Manchester

Top: Lowry Centre; Bottom: Millennium Bridge

Heaton Hall
(3.5 miles/5.5km)
Heaton Park, Prestwich,
M25 9WL
A magnificent 18th century country house with beautifully restored principal rooms.

Surviving the Blitz
(7.5 miles/12km)
Air Raid Shelters
61 Chestergate, Stockport,
SK1 1NE
☎ 0161 474 1940
www.airraidshelters.org.uk
Wander around authentically reconstructed tunnels which provide you with first-hand experience of daily life in 1940s war-torn Britain.

Tatton Park
(16.5 miles/26.5km)
Knutsford, WA16 6QN
☎ 01625 534400
www.tattonpark.org.uk
England's most complete historic estate with mansion, gardens, a traditional working farm, medieval Old Hall, and deer park. There are two lakes, an adventure playground and a self-service restaurant.

Events
Food and Drink Festival

Manchester Jazz Festival

Manchester Pride

S.Percussion

Hotels & Dining
Try the Tourist Information Centre, see Essential Contacts for details.

Something Special

Hilton
303 Deansgate, M3 4LQ
☎ 0161 8701600
www.hilton.co.uk
Conveniently located in the city centre with excellent facilities including a spa, pool and health club. Enjoy international cuisine in the Podium restaurant and a fantastic bar on the 23rd floor with wonderful views over the city.

The Lowry Hotel
50 Dearmans Place, Chapel Wharf,
M3 5LH
☎ 0161 827 4000
www.thelowryhotel.com
A fashionable, award-winning, five-star hotel on the banks of the River Irwell. Here you can dine in a spectacular riverside restaurant or relax in the spa.

Sapporo Teppanyaki Restaurant
Sushi and Noodle Bar, Castlefield,
M3 4JN
☎ 0161 831 98888
www.sapporo.co.uk
Enjoy theatrical cuisine where expert chefs prepare food at your own dedicated grill station.

Grado
New York Street, Piccadilly,
M1 4BD
☎ 0161 238 9790
Stylish Spanish restaurant serving traditional tapas and an eclectic mix of regional and new wave Spanish food.

Essential Contacts

Visitor Information Centre
Town Hall Extension, Lloyd Street,
M60 2LA
☎ 0871 2228223

Salford Tourist Information Centre
The Lowry, Pier 8, M50 3AZ
☎ 0161 848 8601
www.thequays.org.uk

What's on – Manchester Theatres
www.manchestertheatres.com

Cornerhouse
70 Oxford Road, M1 5NH
☎ 0161 200 1500
www.cornerhouse.org
International cinema and visual arts.

Palace Theatre
Oxford Street, M1 6FT
☎ 0870 060 1826
www.manchestertheatres.com

Opera House
Quay Street, M3 3HP
☎ 0161 828 1700

Royal Exchange Theatre
St Ann's Square, M2 7DH
☎ 0161 615 6666

Bridgewater Hall
Lower Moseley Street, M2 3WS
☎ 0161 950 0000

Salford Watersports Centre
15 The Quays, M50 3SQ
☎ 0161 877 7252

Wheel of Manchester
Exchange Square, M3 1BD
☎ 0845 055 6080
For spectacular views of the city.
www.worldtouristattractions.co.uk

Getting There

By Road

South of Telford on A5223 and A4169.

By Rail & Bus

There are trains to Telford Central Station, which is the nearest station to Much Wenlock.

There are national coach/bus operators providing a service to Shrewsbury; you will have to take a local bus service to complete the journey.

Background Briefing

Much Wenlock is a delightful medieval market town full of historical interest, having narrow streets, cobbled passageways, limestone cottages and timber-framed houses. Travel back to a gentler age where it is still possible to sit and watch the world go by. Walk around the town to get a feel for what it was like in earlier days, and see the 15th century John's Cottage, a fine timber-framed cottage with a cobbled front pavement, Church House, and the plain timber-framed Elizabethan building, Raynald's Mansion. Other interesting buildings include Ashfield Hall, once known as St John's Hospital when it was a hostel for "lost and naked beggars"; the cruck-framed St Owen's Well House; the Corn Exchange; the old Police Station and the Squatter's Cottage. Two doors up from the Old Police Station is a half-timbered building called Bastard Hall whose history was televised by Time Team some years ago.

The stone and timber framed Tudor Guildhall is a splendid building with an old stone gaol at the far end; nearby Holy Trinity Church has a nave built in 1150 by the Cluniac monks of Wenlock Priory, and not to be missed are the spectacular ruins of the Priory itself. Follow the Wenlock Olympian Trail, using the bronze plaques mounted in the pavement throughout the town, to discover the significant role of Much Wenlock in the revival of the Modern Olympic Games. The trail ends at the Much Wenlock Museum in the High Street where you will also find the Tourist Information Office. The town bristles with specialist shops, and markets are held in the Corn Exchange on Tuesday, Thursday, Friday and Saturday. A farmers' market is held in the Guildhall on the first and third Friday of the month. Much Wenlock makes a good base to explore the medieval towns of Shrewsbury, Ludlow and Bridgnorth or to visit the award-winning Ironbridge Gorge Museums. Walkers can enjoy rambles through the hills of the Cardingmill Valley (NT), Wenlock Edge or the Long Mynd.

Places to Visit

Wenlock Priory (EH)

TF13 6HS

☎ 01952 727466

The dramatic 12th century ruins of a church and cloistral buildings belonging to the Cluniac Priory. Considerable remains are left of the 350ft long church, including the north and south transepts and parts of the nave. The Priory has delightful grounds and a collection of topiary. The audio tour relates its turbulent history, lasts approximately thirty-five minutes and is included in the admission price.

Much Wenlock Museum

The Memorial, Hall High Street, TF13 6HR

☎ 01952 727679

The museum has displays of local memorabilia, geological history and selected artefacts from the Wenlock Olympian Society.

Wenlock Pottery

Shineton Street, TF13 6HT

☎ 01952 727600

An interesting visit with a ceramic cafe where you can paint your own plates.

The Edge Arts Centre

Farley Road, TF13 6NB

☎ 01952 728509

www.edgeartscentre.co.uk

An arts centre with weekly cinema screenings, performances, workshops and art gallery.

Attractions Nearby

Ironbridge Gorge Museums

(5.5 miles/9km)

Coalbrookdale, Telford, TF8 7DQ

☎ 01952 432166

www.ironbridge.org.uk

Ten amazing museums in one valley including Blist Hill where you can meet the Victorians in a recreated Victorian town, Broseley Pipe Works, Coalbrookdale Museum of Iron, Coalport China Museum, Ironbridge and Tollhouse and Jackfield Tile Museum.

The Edge Adventure Activities

(1.5 miles/2.5km)

Walton Grange, TF13 6PP

☎ 01952 727491

www.theedgeadventure.co.uk

Offers a range of activities including quad biking, grass boarding and archery.

Benthall Hall

(4 miles/6.5km)

Broseley, TF12 5RX

☎ 01952 882159

Handsome 16th century house, situated on a plateau above the gorge of the Severn, with restored kitchen and plantsman's gardens.

Buildwas Abbey (EH)

(3.5 miles/5.5km)

Buildwas, TF8 7BW

Left – Right: The Priory; Cliff Railway; Bridgnorth Castle

☎ 01952 433274

Impressive ruins of a Cistercian abbey.

Shipton Hall
Shipton, Much Wenlock
☎ 01746 785225
An exquisite specimen of Elizabethan architecture set in a quaint old fashioned garden.

Wonderland Telford
(11 miles/17.5km)
Telford Town Park, Telford, TF3 4AY
☎ 01952 591 633
www.wonderlandtelford.com
A children's entertainment venue.

Bridgnorth Attractions
(8.5 miles/13.5km)
Bridgnorth Castle & Gardens, Castle Hill, Bridgnorth, WV16 4AL
A few remains of a Norman castle with spectacular views over the Severn Valley from the surrounding gardens and nearby Castle Walk.

Bridgnorth Cliff Railway
6A Castle Terrace, Bridgnorth, WV16 4AH
☎ 01746 762052
www.bridgnorthcliffrailway.co.uk
The oldest and steepest inland funicular railway in England.

Daniels Mill
Eardington, Bridgnorth, WV16 5JL
☎ 01746 762753
Picturesque working water mill with 38ft cast iron waterwheel.

Dudmaston Hall
Quatt, Bridgnorth, WV15 6QN
☎ 01746 780866

17th century mansion with art collection, lakeside garden and estate.

Rays Farm Country Matters
Billingsley, Bridgnorth, WV16 6PF
☎ 01299 841255
www.raysfarm.com

Events

Much Wenlock Festival
Art, drama and music events staged every two years (2008 next one).

Wenlock Annual Olympian Games

Hotels & Dining
Try the local Tourist Information Centre, see Essential Contacts for details.

Something Special

The Raven Hotel
Barrow Street, Much Wenlock, TF13 6 EN
☎ 01952 727251
A 17th century coaching Inn offering fine food and beautiful rooms. The restaurant is set in what is believed to be the town's original 15th century almshouses and overlooks a delightful inner courtyard.

Haughton Hall
Haughton Lane, Shifnal, TF11 8HG
☎ 01952 468300
www.haughtonhall.com
The hall dates from 1718 and is set in extensive grounds and gardens. Guests have access to the Leisure Club with a 15m heated swimming pool with separate spa, children's pool, fully equipped gymnasium,

steam room, sauna and the latest in solariums. Outdoors there is a nine hole par 3 golf course, a well stocked coarse fishing pool and an outdoor tennis court. The hotel also offers a wide range of beauty, mind and body treatments.

Landmark Trust
Langley Gatehouse, nr. Acton Burnell
C.1610 gatehouse, sleeps six. Mainly half-timbered.

The White House
Aston Munslow
Sleeps eight.

Ironbridge House
Ironbridge
Situated next to the bridge. Sleeps 4.

Plume of Feathers
Harley, Much Wenlock, SY5 6LP
☎ 01952 727360
17th century inn nestling under the Wenlock Edge enjoying stunning views across the valley. The restaurant is renowned for its good food, using fresh local ingredients as well as a daily fresh fish menu.

The Fox
46 High Street, Much Wenlock, TF13 6AD
☎ 01952 727292
www.the-fox-inn.co.uk
Wonderful food in pleasant surroundings.

Essential Contacts

Visitor Information Centre
The Museum, High Street, TF13 6HR
☎ 01952 727679
www.shropshiretourism.info

Gateshead Millennium Bridge and Tyne Bridge

Getting There

By Road

Easily accessed off the A1 from north or south.

By Rail & Bus

Newcastle is on the East Coast mainline and is accessible from around the country although you may need to change trains to complete your journey.

The main coach/bus operators offer a service to Newcastle although you may need to make changes to complete your journey.

Background Briefing

Newcastle is an exciting destination with a lively atmosphere having an excellent choice of cafes, restaurants and wine bars. The city is renowned for the variety and quality of its shops and often has weekend visitors from Scandinavia intent on a little retail therapy. Newcastle's nightlife is legendary so head for the Quayside, Bigg Market or Jesmond for a huge variety of bars, clubs and

entertainment venues. Alternatively visit a cinema, the Victorian Theatre Royal or listen to classical music at City Hall or The Sage, go to the races or take a sightseeing cruise on the river; there's something to suit all tastes here.

However this modern city retains much of the past and a large portion of the medieval town walls can still be seen. Explore the Norman keep, one of the finest in England, and climb the 134 steps to the top for breathtaking panoramic views. The city centre is compact making it easy to explore the wide streets on foot and to admire the elegant Georgian buildings, Victorian architecture and spacious squares.

Don't miss the Regency style buildings in Grey Street, the 17th century Alderman Fenwick's House in Pilgrim Street, Pugin's Cathedral Church of St Mary, the 14th century St Nicholas' Cathedral and Bessie Surtees' House near the Quayside. Additionally Newcastle has a cornucopia of art galleries and museums guaranteed

to interest and intrigue adults and children alike. Also worth a look is the Blue Carpet art installation situated outside the Laing Gallery which features blue tiles made from glass and resin.

A walk along the banks of the Tyne will take you past other examples of public art as well as pleasant places to stop for a meal or a drink. Away from the city centre is Blackfriars, a former monastery dating from the 13th century, where you can relax in quieter surroundings whilst enjoying the craft shops or award-winning restaurant. One of the best ways to appreciate all that Newcastle has to offer is to pick up a walking trail leaflet from the Visitor Information Centre or use the city's hop-on hop-off bus service which starts from the railway station. Further a field is the fine golden sand of Longsands beach, wonderful gardens, historic halls and Roman forts and museums, not forgetting the beautiful Northumbrian countryside and the northeast coastline.

Place to Visit

The Castle Keep

Saint Nicholas Street, Castle Garth, NE1 1RQ

☎ 0191 2327938

museums.ncl.ac.uk

One of the finest examples of a Norman keep in the country, built during the reign of Henry II. Explore the chapel, garrison room, great hall and chambers then climb to the top for stunning views over the city.

Grainger Town

The buildings in this historic, regenerated area of the city will delight the eye. Discover classical Georgian and Victorian architecture and stroll along the elegantly

curved Grey Street, once voted the best street in England by Radio 4 listeners.

Centre for Life

Times Square, NE1 4EP

☎ 0191 243 8210

www.life.org.uk

Visit this fascinating venue, full of interactive, audiovisual and hands on activities, where science comes to life. Ride the state of the art motion simulator or come face to face with your 90 year old self, discover your origins and your future. If you visit in winter there is an outdoor ice rink in Times Square.

Bessie Surtees' House (EH)

41–44 Sandhill, NE1 3JF

☎ 0191 269 1200

A well-preserved example of Jacobean domestic architecture, now the regional office of EH.

Discovery Museum

Blandford House, Blandford Square, NE1 4JA

☎ 0191 232 6789

www.twmuseums.org.uk

Find out about life on Tyneside using numerous hands-on interactives.

Gateshead Quays

www.gateshead-quays.com

A new cultural quarter with riverside walks, fantastic architectural buildings, and public displays of art.

Laing Art Gallery

New Bridge Street, NE1 8AJ

☎ 0191 232 7734

www.twmuseums.org.uk

Seven Stories

The Centre for Children's Books 30 Lime Street, Ouseburn Valley, NE1 2PQ

☎ 0845 271 0777

www.sevenstories.org.uk

Dedicated to children's books with

unconventional exhibitions and entertaining events and activities.

Attractions Nearby

Gibside (NT)

(9.5 miles/15km)

Near Rowlands Gill, Burnopfield NE16 6BG

☎ 01207 541820

A stunning 18th century landscape garden with peaceful woodland and riverside walks. Visit the Palladian Chapel, with its unusual three-tiered pulpit, and other decorative garden buildings. Gibside is the ancestral estate of the Bowes-Lyon family.

Segedunum Roman Fort

(5 miles/8km)

Buddle Street, Wallsend, NE28 6HR

☎ 0191 236 9347

www.twmuseums.org.uk

This 'strong fort' once housed 600 Roman soldiers and is the most excavated fort along Hadrian's Wall. There is a large interactive museum and a high viewing tower where you can look out over the World Heritage Site.

Arbeia Roman Fort & Museum

(12.5 miles/20km)

Baring Street, South Shields, NE33 2BB

☎ 0191 456 1369

www.twmuseums.org.uk

Belsay Hall, Castle and Gardens (EH)

(15 miles/24km)

Belsay, Northumberland, NE20 0DX

☎ 01661 881636

Kirkley Hall

(12 miles/19.5km)

Ponteland, Northumberland, NE20 0AQ

☎ 01670 841 235

www.kirkleyhall.co.uk

Top - Bottom: Tynemouth Prior and castle an English Heritage Site in Tyne and Wear; Blacksmith Needle in Quayside; Tyne Bridge and Quayside

Path Head Water Mill
(12 miles/19.5km)
Summerhill, Blaydon NE21 4SP
☎ 0191 414 6288
A restored 18th century working
water mill.

Tynemouth Priory (EH)
(10 miles/16km)
Tynemouth, NE30 4BZ
☎ 0191 257 1090

Events
Beer Festival

Community Green Festival

Dancing the World
(International Dance Festival)

Eat Festival
(Food)

Evolution Music Festival
(The biggest music festival in the
northwest)

**Newcastle Gateshead Comedy
Festival**

Hotels & Dining
Try the Tourist Information Centre,
see Essential Contacts for details.

Something Special
The Vermont
Castle Garth, NE1 1RQ
0191 233 1010
www.vermont-hotel.com
The Vermont is a luxury four star
independent city centre hotel,
located next to the Castle, overlooking the Cathedral, The Sage
Gateshead, and the Tyne and Gateshead Millennium Bridge.

The Caledonian Hotel
Osborne Road, Jesmond,
NE2 2AT
☎ 0191 281 7881
www.caledonian-hotel-newcastle.
com
The Caledonian Hotel is located
in the heart of Jesmond, a chic and
leafy area, only one mile from the

Overview of Newcastle

city centre. An extensive refurbishment combines a classic Georgian
facade with a stylish contemporary
interior.

**Newcastle Marriott
Gosforth Park Hotel**
High Gosforth Park, NE3 5HN
☎ 0191 236 4111
www.newcastlemarriottgos
forthpark.co.uk

Landmark Trust
The Banqueting House, Gibside
(One mile ssouthwest of New-
castle)
Lovely building built around 1746,
set in Gibside park. Sleeps six.

Morpeth Castle, Morpeth
(Fifteen miles north of Newcastle)
Gatehouse to the AD1200 castle.
Sleeps yourself and six retainers,
above the town.

Black Door
32 Clayton Street West,
NE1 5DZ
☎ 0191 261 6295
www.blackdoorgroup.co.uk
Classic French cuisine in an elegant
Georgian building.

**BALTIC Rooftop
Restaurant**
South Shore Road, Gateshead
Quays, NE8 3BA
☎ 0191 440 4949

A superb dining experience with
spectacular views of Newcastle,
Gateshead and the Millennium
Bridge.

Essential Contacts
**Guildhall Visitor
Information Centre**
Quayside, NE1 3AF
☎ 0191 277 8000

Boat Trips
River Escapes
☎ 01670 785666/785777
www.riverescapes.co.uk

City Hall
Northumberland Road, NE1 8SF
Box Office 0191 2612606

Newcastle City Tours
☎ 07780 958679
www.newcastlecitytours.co.uk

Newcastle Racecourse
High Gosforth Park NE3 5HP
☎ 0191 236 2020

The Sage
St Mary's Square, Gateshead Quays,
NE8 2JR
Ticket Office ☎ 0191 443 4661

Theatre Royal
Grey Street, NE1 6BR
Booking Office ☎ 0870 905 5060
www.theatreroyal.co.uk

Norwich's 11th century castle

Getting There

By Road

A11 from the southwest; from the west A47; from the south or north take the A1, pick up the A47 at Peterborough.

By Rail & Bus

Norwich is well served by the rail network.

There are several coach/bus companies offering a service into Norwich although it may be necessary to make changes to get there.

Background Briefing

Norwich with its ancient buildings and remains of a city wall is the most complete medieval city in Britain. It is known as the city of churches as there are over thirty medieval churches within the city walls alone. Many are still open for worship but others have been converted to other uses. There are hundreds of historic buildings to find while wandering through medieval streets, lanes and alleys in the city. Norwich has historic half-timbered houses, Georgian and Victorian buildings, Art Nouveau and Art Deco architecture, a Guildhall dating from the early 15th century, a plethora of museums and art galleries and fantastic shops.

In Norwich ancient and modern sit side-by-side enabling the visitor to enjoy the best of both worlds.

Specialist shops abound in the medieval alleys and back streets of the Norwich Lanes and in the picturesque, cobbled Elm Hill, which has a wide variety of shops, bars and restaurants. Norwich is in the top five places to shop in the UK; one has the added attraction of being able to shop to a backdrop of stunning architecture.

The market, which stands below the castle, is the largest open-air market in the country and is open six days a week. While in Norwich visit the magnificent Norman Cathedral and Castle, enjoy a night out at one of the theatres, dine in a mouth-watering restaurant or wander along the Wensum riverside walk and see Pulls Ferry, once a

Norwich Cathedral

15th century water gate. You can see the city from an open-top bus, a boat on the river or by joining a guided walking tour. If you need a break from the multitude of attractions in the city there are several parks and gardens where you can enjoy peace and serenity. Why not visit the Broads, the most popular inland waterways in Europe, where you will see herons, coots, ducks and swans at close quarters.

Places to Visit

Norwich Cathedral
62 The Close, NR1 4EH
☎ 01603 218321
This beautiful, honey-coloured Norman cathedral has spectacular and awe-inspiring architecture, a towering spire, magnificent medieval paintings and frescos, medieval misericords and unique 14th century roof bosses depicting biblical scenes. The two-storey monastic cloisters are the largest in England, and the cathedral close has several fine ancient gateways and a rich mix of domestic architecture.

Norwich Castle Museum & Art Gallery
Castle Meadow, NR1 3JU
☎ 01603 493625
The 12th century Castle is one of the finest Norman secular buildings in Europe. Once a royal castle it is now a museum with nationally important collections of art, archaeology and natural history.

Cow Tower (EH)
Near Cathedral
☎ 01603 213434
One of the earliest purpose-built 14th century artillery blockhouses, it commands a strategic point in Norwich's city defences.

Strangers' Hall
Charing Cross, NR2 4AL
☎ 01603 667229

One of the oldest and most fascinating buildings in Norwich, once the home of wealthy merchants and Mayors. See the Tudor great hall, the fine Georgian dining room and the magnificent stone-vaulted undercroft. Outside is a lavender-filled garden.

Other Places to Visit

Dragon Hall
115–123 King Street, NR1 1QE
☎ 01603 663922
www.dragonhall.org
A medieval trading hall, built in about 1430 and one of the most important historic buildings in Norwich.

Inspire Discovery Centre
St Michaels Church, Oak Street,
☎ 01303 612612
www.inspirediscoverycentre.com
Inspire is a hands-on science centre housed in a medieval church.

Roman Catholic Cathedral
Unthank Road, NR2 2PA
☎ 01603 624615
www.stjohncathedral.co.uk
A magnificent example of 19th century gothic revival featuring some of the finest 19th century stained glass in Europe.

Royal Norfolk Regimental Museum
Shirehall, Market Avenue
NR1 3JQ
☎ 01603 493649
www.rnrm.org.uk

Sainsbury Centre for Visual Arts
University of East Anglia, Earlham Road, NR4 7TJ
☎ 01603 593199
www.scva.org.uk
An inspirational public art gallery and museum.

The Bridewell
Bridewell Alley, NR2 1AQ
☎ 01603 629127

Top – Bottom: Ornate face of clock at Norwich Cathedral; Window of old police office; Modern structure in front of ancient castle; Norwich Cathedral interior

Once a prison for women and beggars but now a delightful museum.

The Plantation Garden
4 Earlham Road, NR2 3DB
☎ 01603 621868
A wonderfully restored Victorian town garden just 600 yards from the city centre.

Landmark Visitors Guide: Norfolk & the Broads; ISBN: 9781843063271; £7.99

Attractions Nearby

Banham Zoo
(24 miles/38.5km)
The Grove, Banham, NR16 2HE
www.banhamzoo.co.uk

Blickling Hall (NT)
(14.5 miles/23km)
Blickling, nr Norwich,
NR11 6NF
☎ 01263 738030
A magnificent Jacobean house with gardens and park. Famed for its long gallery, fine tapestries, paintings and rare books.

Felbrigg Hall, Garden & Park (NT)
(23 miles/37km)
Felbrigg NR11 8PR
☎ 01263 83744
One of the most elegant country houses in East Anglia. Remarkable Stuart architecture and fine Georgian interior.

Wymondham Heritage Museum
(11.5 miles/18.5km)
10 The Bridewell, Norwich Road, Wymondham, NR18 0NS
☎ 01953 600205
email: wymondhamheritage museum.co.uk

Wymondham Abbey
Church Street, Wymondham, NR18 0PH
☎ 01953 607062
www.wymondhamabbey.nildram. co.uk

Events

DumDuckerDum Music Festival

East Coast Jazz Festival

Norfolk and Norwich Festival

Norwich Beer Festival

Norwich Fringe Festival

The Bidwells Norwich & Norfolk Food Festival

Spring and Autumn International Literary Festivals

Hotels & Dining

Try the local Tourist Information Centre, see Essential Contacts for details.

Something Special

De Vere Dunstan Hall
Ipswich Road, NR14 8PQ
☎ 01508 470444
www.devere-hotels.com
An imposing country house hotel set in 170 acres of landscaped gardens with spa facilities including sauna, solarium and jacuzzi and a superb range of leisure facilities.

Park Farm Country Hotel
Hethersett, NR9 3DL
☎ 01603 810264
www.parkfarm-hotel.co.uk
An exclusive country house hotel is set in 200 acres of beautiful landscaped gardens and farmland. Georgian restaurant offering fine traditional cuisine. The hotel has a superb leisure complex, including an indoor pool, a fully equipped gymnasium, Jacuzzi, steam room, aerobics studio, beauticians and hairdressing salon.

Marriott Sprowston Manor Hotel and Country Club
Wroxham Road, NR7 8RP1
☎ 01603 410871
An award-winning hotel with a championship par 71 18 hole golf course, luxury spa, pool and fitness centre.

Brummells Seafood Restaurant
7 Magdalen Street, NR3 1LE
☎ 01603 625555
www.brummells.co.uk

Merchants of Colegate
30–32 Colegate, NR3 1BG
☎ 01603 611711/766566
Good food and wine in an historic area of Norwich.

Pulse Cafe Bar
The Old Fire Station Stables, Labour in Vain Yard, Guildhall Hill
☎ 01603 765377
Wonderful funky vegetarian food prepared from organic produce.

St Benedict's Restaurant
9 St Benedicts St, NR2 4PE
☎ 01603 765377
A classy restaurant serving a mix of traditional and modern food using locally sourced, often organic and free range produce.

Essential Contacts

Tourist Information Centre
The Forum, Millennium Plain
NR2 1TF
☎ 01603 727927

City Boat Tours
☎ 0160 0701701
www.cityboats.co.uk

Guided walking tours
Contact Tourist Information

Theatre Royal
Theatre Street, NR2 1RL
☎ 01603 630000

Norwich Playhouse Theatre
42–58, St Georges Street,
NR3 1AB
☎ 01603 612580

Open Top Bus Tours
☎ 0871666000
www.city-sightseeing.com

Maddermarket Theatre
St Johns Alley, NR2 1DR
☎ 01603 620917

Norwich Arts Centre
St Benedict's Street, NR2 4PG
☎ 01603 660352

Oxford, Oxfordshire

Top: All Souls College; **Bottom:** View of Oxford

Getting There

By Road

M40 south, J9, A34; M40 north J8, A40; from southwest A34 or west A40.

By Rail & Bus

Oxford is well served by the rail network.

There are several coach/bus companies offering a service into Oxford although it may be necessary to make changes to get there.

Background Briefing

Oxford is a town like no other; it is stunningly beautiful, in a unique riverside setting and renowned all over the world for its universities. It is a compact city whose streets radiate from the Carfax Tower with most of the academic buildings within easy walking distance. There are numerous museums full

of national treasures, making it difficult to choose which ones to visit. The Ashmolean is the oldest museum in England and one of the best and the Pitt Rivers is always a fascinating place to visit.

Perhaps the best way to explore the city is to take a guided walking tour; the University and City Tour will lead you through the heart of the historic city centre. The tour uncovers the history of Oxford and its universities and describes the architecture and traditions of its most famous buildings and institutions. A good view of the famous colleges can be had from the top of St Mary's Church tower. Stand on the Venetian 'Bridge of Sighs' in New College Lane and look to your left to see the most famous group of buildings in Oxford. Oxford has many literary links and has often been used for film and TV locations. Fans of Colin Dexter can follow the

Inspector Morse Tour which visits the scenes of Inspector Morse's best known cases.

Christ Church College, the setting for Hogwarts in the Harry Potter films, is the largest college in Oxford and the only college in the world with a cathedral within its walls. One of the former pupils was Lewis Carroll. Away from the bustling city centre full of individual shops, restaurants, bars and cafes are quieter areas where you can relax. Take a trip in a punt along the River Cherwell, wander through rural walkways in Christ Church Meadows or explore the entrancing Botanic Gardens, opposite Magdalen College, where there are beautiful flowerbeds and greenhouses filled with rare plants.

Entertainment is on offer at the Apollo Theatre and the refurbished Georgian Oxford Playhouse, and classical music concerts are held at the Sheldonian Theatre and Christ Church Cathedral. There is something for everyone in Oxford.

Places to visit

Carfax Tower

Queen Street, OX1 1ER
☎ 01865 792653

There are wonderful views of Oxford's 'dreaming spires' from the top of the tower, which was part of the 14th century St Martin's Church. The spires seen can be identified from a display. Don't miss the clock on the east side of the tower which has mechanical figures known as 'quarter boys' which hammer out the quarter hours on bells. The name Carfax derives from the French carrefour, or crossroads.

Christ Church College

St Aldate's, OX1 1DP
☎ 01865 276492

The oldest college in Oxford and the only college with a cathedral

Top – Bottom: Oxford Radcliffe Library; Bridge of Sighs; View of Oxford, across the top of the Brasenose and Exeter colleges; Aeriel view of Oxford; Christ Church - used in Harry Potter films as Gryffindor House

within its walls. This beautiful building has a fascinating history and makes a memorable visit. Christ Church was founded in 1525 and re-endowed in 1546 by Henry VIII. At 9.05pm every night you will hear the sound of Great Tom, the loudest bell in town, which chimes 101 times in the tower designed by Christopher Wren. The bell was taken from the 12th century Osney Abbey after the Reformation. Christ Church Memorial Gardens are surrounded by Christ Church Meadows running down to the Rivers Cherwell and Thames.

The Ashmolean Museum

Beaumont Street, OX1 2HP
☎ 01865 278000
www.ashmolean.org

The museum is located in a neo-Gothic style building designed by Charles Robert Cockerell in 1845. The Ashmolean was established in 1683 but at that time the museum was in another building in Broad Street. Collections of national and international importance are housed in the museum. They range over four millennia – from the civilisations of ancient Egypt, Greece and Rome to Renaissance Europe.

Modern Art Oxford

30 Pembroke Street, OX1 1BP
☎ 01865 722733
www.modernartoxford.org.uk

This leading art gallery was established in 1965 and is renowned for the quality of its exhibitions, activities and publications. Innovative programmes enable visitors to participate in and engage with contemporary art.

Oxford Castle Unlocked

44–46 Oxford Castle, New Road, OX1 1AY
☎ 01865 260666
www.oxfordcastleunlocked.co.uk

A new attraction allowing visitors, for the first time, to walk through ancient buildings and experience stories connecting real people to extraordinary events.

University of Oxford Botanic Garden

Rose Lane, OX1 4AZ
☎ 01865 286690
www.botanic-garden.ox.ac.uk

The oldest botanic garden in Britain, full of stunning plants and beautiful borders, inspired by gardening styles around the world. Over 6,000 different species of plants can be seen in the walled garden, glasshouses, rock and water gardens.

Pitt Rivers Museum

South Parks Road, OX2 6PN
☎ 01865 270927

The University of Oxford's museum of anthropology and world archaeology was founded in 1884 following a gift to the university from General Pitt Rivers.

Radcliffe Camera

Radcliffe Square
☎ 01865 277000

Although not open to the public and now the main reading room of the Bodleian Library, the circular dome and drum of the Radcliffe Camera is one of the most distinctive landmarks in the city and well worth a visit.

Museum at Bate Collection of Musical Instruments

Faculty of Music, St Aldate's, OX1 1DB
☎ 01865 276139
www.bate.ox.ac.uk

England's most comprehensive collection of European woodwind, brass and percussion instruments.

Museum of Oxford

St Aldate's, OX1 1DB
☎ 01865 252761

This fascinating museum has galleries looking at the life of the city from Prehistoric times to the present day.

Museum of the History of Science

Broad Street, OX1 3AZ

☎ 01865 277280

www.mhs.ox.ac.uk

The Old Ashmolean building in Broad Street houses an unrivalled collection of historic scientific instruments.

St Mary the Virgin Church

High Street, OX1 4AH

www.university-church.ox.ac.uk

Fine views of Oxford's famous skyline can be seen from the top of the 14th century tower. The church dates from differing periods; the nave was rebuilt in the early 16th century in the Perpendicular style.

University Museum of Natural History

Parks Road, OX1 3PW

☎ 01865 272950

www.oum.ox.ac.uk

In a spectacular neo-Gothic building the museum houses scientific collections of zoological, entomological and geological specimens. Don't miss the Oxfordshire dinosaurs, the dodo, and the swifts in the tower.

Attractions Nearby

Blenheim Palace

(9 miles/14.5km)

Woodstock, OX20 1PX

☎ 01993 811091

www.blenheimpalace.com

This baroque masterpiece was built for the first Duke of Marlborough and is now a World Heritage Site.

Didcot Railway Centre

(15 miles/24km)

Didcot, OX11 7NJ

☎ 01235-817200

www.didcotrailwaycentre.org

Unique collection of Great Western Steam engines. They hold various events throughout the year.

Events

Many Festivals and Fairs are held in Oxford each year. Contact Tourist Information or visit www.visitoxford.org for details.

Fringe Festival

Literary Festival

Folk Festival

Visual Arts Festival

Chamber Music Festival

Medieval Fair

St Giles Fair

Hotels & Dining

Try the Tourist Information Centre, see Essential Contacts for details.

Something Special

Oxford Spires Four Pillars Hotel

Abingdon Road, OX1 4PS

☎ 01865 324324

www.four-pillars.co.uk

Just a short riverside walk away from the centre of Oxford. The hotel has a leisure club with pool, gym and spa.

The Old Parsonage Hotel

1 Banbury Road, OX2 6NN

☎ 01865 310210

www.oldparsonage-hotel.co.uk

Luxury accommodation a short walk from the city centre in a peaceful setting with roof-top herb garden. The interior has the atmosphere of a private members' club and can claim Oscar Wilde as a former resident.

Macdonald Randolph Hotel

Beaumont Street, OX1 2LN

☎ 0844 879 9132

www.randolph-hotel.com

Five star hotel in the heart of the city, opposite the Ashmolean Museum, complete with a spa.

Landmark Trust

The Old Parsonage, Mill Lane, Iffley, Oxford

Dates from around 1500, with a riverside garden. Sleeps six.

The Steward's House

St Michaels Street, Oxford

Sleeps two.

The Big Bang

124 Walton Street, Jericho, Oxford, OX2 6AH

☎ 01865 511441

www.thebigbangoxford.co.uk

Award-winning bangers and mash with a difference. Top quality gourmet sausages, homemade pies and a variety of flavoured mash.

Moya

Slovak restaurant and cocktail bar. 97 St. Clements St, Oxford, OX4 1AR

☎ 01865 200111

www.moya-oxford.co.uk

Essential Contacts

Oxford Information Centre

15/16 Broad St, Oxford, OX1 3AS

☎ 01865 726871

www.oxfordeguide.com

Contact the information centre for details of walking tours.

Bill Spectre's Oxford Ghost Trail

☎ 07941 041811

www.ghosttrail.org

Open-top bus tours

City Sightseeing Oxford

☎ 01865 790522

Oxford River Cruises

34 West Street, Osney Island

☎ 0845 2269396

Oxford River Cruises offers scheduled trips, private charters and boat hire on Oxford's magical waterways.

Cherwell Boathouse

Bardwell Road

☎ 01865 515978

Riverside restaurant and over seventy hand-built punts available for hire.

Getting there

By Road

M5 J31, A38.

By Rail & Bus

There are good services to Plymouth from around the country, you may have to change trains or coach to complete your journey.

Background Briefing

This historic seafaring port with its rich maritime heritage combines with a vibrant modern city centre to provide an ideal venue for a short break. Stroll through the Barbican, with its associations with Drake and Raleigh, and discover the Mayflower Steps where the Pilgrim Fathers set sail for America; visit the Black Friars Distillery, home of Plymouth Gin; or immerse yourself in the magic of the National Marine Aquarium with its fantastic attractions.

The narrow streets and alleyways of the Barbican are home to art galleries, museums and a variety of unique and individual shops. Wander along the wide promenade of the Hoe with views of yachts and pleasure cruisers out at sea. The more adventurous might like to take a dip in the elegant restored Art Deco Tinside Lido, which is

Left: Harbour Bridge **Right:** Typical English houses in Plymouth

separated from the sea by just a wall. If you visit in summer take a tour around the battlements of the Royal Citadel, a 17th century fortress, built on the Hoe to defend the coastline from the Dutch.

Visit the Farmers' Market which sets up twice a month, on the second and fourth Saturdays, at the Piazza. Numerous waterborne activities abound where enthusiasts can take part in canoeing, fishing, jet and water skiing, sailing, scuba diving and windsurfing.

Places to Visit

The National Marine Aquarium

Rope Walk, Coxside, PL4 0LF
☎ 01752 600 301
www.national-aquarium.co.uk
This is Britain's biggest aquarium. See the latest satellite images from space and go on a 3D deep-sea journey. There are over 3,000 fish and eleven species of sharks.

Saltram (NT)

Plympton, PL7 1UH
☎ 01752 333500
This Georgian mansion with opulent Robert Adam interiors is set in landscaped parkland. Saltram has been used as a film location for Sense and Sensibility. Situated approximately one mile from town.

Other Places to Visit

Black Friars Distillery

60 Southside Street, Barbican, PL1 2LQ
☎ 01752 665292
www.plymouthgin.com

Elizabethan House

32 New Street, The Barbican, PL1 2NA
The furnished home of an Elizabethan sea captain.

Merchant's House

33 St Andrew Street, PL1 2AH
A historic building tucked away down one of the city's oldest streets. The Merchant's House is Plymouth's finest surviving example of a 16th/17th century residence.

Plymouth City Museum & Art Gallery

Drake Circus, PL4 8AJ
☎ 01752 304774
www.plymouth.gov.uk
Only partially open at time of going to press (due to refurbishment).

Plymouth Mayflower Visitor Centre

3–5 The Barbican, PL1 2TR
☎ 01752 306330
Interactive exhibition telling the story of the Mayflower and Plymouth Harbour.

Royal Citadel (EH)

Madeira Road
☎ 01752 775841
A dramatic 17th century fortress. Still in use by the military today. Guided tours only.

Attractions Nearby

Buckland Abbey (NT)

(10 miles/16km)
Yelverton, PL20 6EY
☎ 01822 853607
The home of Elizabethan seafarer Sir Francis Drake, in the beautiful Tavy Valley.

Plymouth lighthouse on the Hoe

Cotehele (NT)
(16.5 miles/26.5km)
St Dominick, nr Saltash,
PL12 6TA
☎ 01579 351346
Tudor house with superb collections of textiles, armour and furniture, set in extensive grounds extended to a quay on the River Tamar.

Morwellham Quay
(20 miles/32km)
Near Tavistock, PL19 8JL
☎ 01822-832766
www.morwellham-quay.co.uk
An award-winning, evocative museum and visitor centre based around the historic port and mine workings on the River Tamar.

Mount Edgcumbe House & Country Park
(13 miles/20.5km)
Cremyll, Torpoint PL10 1HZ
☎ 01752 822236
www.mountedgcumbe.gov.uk
Set in Grade I Cornish gardens within 865 acres of country park on the Rame Peninsula.

Events
Annual Sailing Regatta

The Barbican International Jazz and Blues Festival

British Fireworks Championships

Formula One World Powerboat Championships

Navy Days

Respect Festival

Summer Festival

Volksfest

Hotels & Dining
Try the Tourist Information Centre, see Essential Contacts for details.

Something Special

Copthorne Hotel
Armada Way, PL1 1AR
☎ 01752 224 161

Ideally located in the city centre and close to many attractions. The hotel's Bentleys Brasserie is an award-winning restaurant.

Elfordleigh Hotel
Colebrook, Plympton, PL7 5EB
☎ 01752 336428
www.elfordleigh.co.uk
The peace and tranquillity of an English country house complete with Oasis leisure and spa facilities.

Langdon Court Hotel
Wembury, PL9 0DY
☎ 01752 862 358
www.langdoncourt.com
Tudor mansion set in ten acres of historic gardens, near to Wenbury beach and coastal footpaths.

The New Continental
Milbay Road, PL1 3LD
☎ 01752 220782
www.newcontinental.co.uk
In the city centre within easy walking distance of the Hoe and with excellent leisure facilities.

Landmark Trust
Crown Hill Fort
Part of the Victorian naval defences. Sleeps eight.

Danes Combe Mine
Calstock.
Old copper mine engine house. Sleeps four (nr Cotehele).

Endsleigh
Nr Tavistock
Pond Cottage includes fly fishing pond. Sleeps five. Plymouth 15 miles/24km.

Tanners Restaurant
Prysten House, Finewell Street, PL1 2AE
☎ 01752 252001
www.tannersrestaurant.com
Fine food and wine in a convivial atmosphere.

Bistro Bacchanalia
Dolphin House, Sutton Harbour, PL4 0DW
☎ 01752 254879
A stunning waterside restaurant overlooking the marina.

Essential Contacts

Tourist Information Centre
Within Mayflower Centre, 3–5 The Barbican, PL1 2LR
☎ 01752 306330

Barbican Theatre
Castle Street, PL1 2NJ
☎ 01752 267131

Plymouth Boat Cruises
☎ 01752 822797

Plymouth Pavilions
Millbay Road, PL1 3LF
☎ 0845 146 1460
www.plymouthpavilions.com
Main venue for theatre and comedy together with ice rink and pool.

Tamar Cruising & Cremyll Ferry
☎ 01752 822105

Theatre Royal & Drum Theatre
Royal Parade, PL1 2TR
☎ 01752 267222
www.theatreroyal.com

Mount Batten Centre
70 Lawrence Road, Mount Batten, Plymstock, PL9 9SJ
☎ 01752 404567
www.mount-batten-centre.com
All kinds of water sports.

Landmark Visitors Guide: Devon;
ISBN: 9781843063735;
£9.99

Landmark Visitors Guide: Cornwall & the Isles of Scilly;
ISBN: 9781843063711;
£9.99

Rochester, Kent

Getting There

By Road

From the south – A2 to J with the M2, take the left-hand fork into Rochester and Strood.

From the north – M5 to A2 exit. Follow the A2 to J with M2, take the left-hand fork into Rochester and Strood.

By Rail & Bus

There are mainline services from around the country although you may have to make changes to complete the journey

Nearest coach station is Gillingham, to where main coach/bus operators offer a service from around the country.

Background Briefing

Rochester is a lovely town where it is easy to walk through historic streets to visit the castle, cathedral and museums. The town exudes Victorian charm; the High Street, lined with specialist shops and historic buildings, is perfect for a spot of relaxed browsing. The town has an eclectic range of restaurants featuring international cuisine. It is a town beloved by Charles Dickens and memories of the distinguished author are everywhere, as many of the buildings featured in his novels can still be seen. Restoration House, which featured as the home of Estella and Miss Faversham in Great Expectations, may be visited in the summer months.

The Guildhall Museum has a Dickens Discovery Room and you can follow in Dickens' footsteps on a self-guided walking trail available from the Visitor Centre. Joining a circular guided walk will provide an excellent introduction to the town. They start from the Visitor Centre in the High Street and are organised by the City of Rochester Society. During the summer there are concerts in the castle gardens and an annual Sweep's Festival takes place over the May Day bank holiday, when local sweeps, Morris dancers and folk groups from all over the UK join in the fun. The annual Dickens Festival is a traditional celebration of the Victorian era. Rochester is ideally placed for visiting numerous attractions in the immediate surrounding area, including the Historic Dockyard at Chatham and the Tudor artillery fortress of Upnor Castle.

Places to Visit

Rochester Cathedral

High Street, ME1 1JY

☎ 01634 843366

email: enquiries@rochester cathedral.org

www.rochestercathedral.org

The second oldest in England, founded in AD604. Bishop Gundulph, William the Conqueror's architect, began the construction of the present building in 1080 and it was finally consecrated as a cathedral in 1130. It is an inspirational place to visit with magnificent Norman and Gothic architecture and fine Romanesque facades together with an atmospheric crypt.

Rochester Castle (EH)

ME1 1SW

☎ 01634 402276

This fine example of a Norman fortress was begun in 1087; it is one of the best-preserved examples of Norman architecture in England. Its great keep, towering over the town, has breathtaking views from the top. The pleasant grassy castle grounds are free to enter and make an ideal picnic spot with splendid views of the river and the nearby cathedral.

Other Places to Visit

Guildhall Museum

High Street, ME1 1PY

☎ 01634 848717

A timeline through Medway's history; includes the Dickens Discovery Room and The Hulk Experience (military hospitals and floating prisons).

Restoration House & Gardens

17–19 Crow Lane ME1 1RF

☎ 01634 848520

www.restorationhouse.co.uk

Restoration House is a unique survival of a city mansion. Situated in the heart of historic Rochester the house takes its name from the stay of King Charles II on the eve of the Restoration.

Six Poor Travellers House

High Street, Rochester, ME1 1LX

This Tudor charity house was founded in 1563 by local MP Richard Watts to provide free lodgings for poor travellers. The name of the house derives from the poor travellers who were provided one night's lodging in the six bedrooms built to the rear of this almshouse in the 16th century.

Attractions Nearby

Dickens World

(2 miles/3.5km)

Leviathan Way,

Chatham Maritime, ME4 4LL

☎ 01634 890012

www.dickensworld.co.uk

Take a fascinating journey through Dickens' lifetime as you step back into Dickensian England, immersed in the urban streets, sounds and smells of the 19th century.

Historic Dockyard

(2 miles/3.5km)

Dock Road, Chatham, ME4 4TZ

☎ 01634 823800

www.chdt.org.uk
Important maritime heritage site covering eighty acres and dating back over 400 years. Historic architecture and ships, sail and rope making, museum galleries, interactive exhibitions and much more.

Medway Heritage Centre
(2 miles/3.5km)
Dock Road, Chatham, ME4 4SH
☎ 01634 408437
The Medway Heritage Centre, formerly St Mary's Church, tells the story of the River Medway using photographs, paintings, models and artefacts.

Royal Engineers Museum
(3 miles/5km)
Prince Arthur Road, Gillingham, ME4 4UG
☎ 01634 822839
www.remuseum.org.uk
The tale of Britain's military engineers in twenty-six galleries. Innumerable fascinating items including Gordon's mementoes, weapons from Rorke's Drift and Wellington's map of Waterloo.

Temple Manor (EH)
(2 miles/3.5km)
Knight Road, Strood, ME2 2AH
☎ 01634 402276
13th century Knights Templar hall house, with some 17th century extensions. Its original purpose was to provide lodgings and fresh horses for members of this Order on their way to and from the Crusades.

Upnor Castle (EH)
(3 miles/5km)
High Street, Upnor, ME2 4XG
☎ 01634 718742
Tudor artillery fortress set in a picturesque village with stunning views across the Medway.

Events
Summer Concerts in the castle gardens

Sweep's Festival – May Day
A traditional, colourful and lively festival annual festival when local chimney sweeps, Morris sides and folk groups from all over the UK join in the fun. See website for more details:
www.medway.gov.uk

Dickens Festival – June
A spectacular event of colour, costume and entertainment. See website for more details:
www.medway.gov.uk

Contact Visitor Centre for further information.

Hotels & Dining
Try the local Tourist Information Centre, see Essential Contacts for more details.

Something Special
Gordon House Hotel
91 High Street, ME1 1LX
☎ 01634 831000
www.gordonhousehotel.net
A 17th century hotel in the heart of the historic city.

Bridgewood Manor
Bridgewood Roundabout, Walderslade Woods, Chatham, ME5 9AX
☎ 01634 201333
www.qhotels.co.uk
Fine food and excellent service at the four star Bridgewood Manor where guests can enjoy the indoor heated pool, well-equipped gymnasium and luxury spa offering a range of body and beauty treatments.

Elizabeth's of Eastgate
154 High Street
☎ 01634 843472
www.elizabethsofeastgate.co.uk
Serves fine food and wine in wonderful Tudor buildings dating back to the 16th century with many original features still intact.

Topes
60 High Street

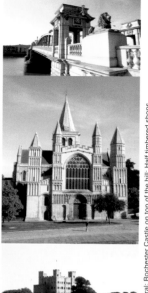

☎ 01634 845270
A modern European restaurant serving a lunch-time brassiere menu and an á la carte dinner menu.

Essential Contacts
Visitor Information Centre
95 High Street, Kent, ME1 1LX
☎ 01634 843666
www.medway.gov.uk/tourism

Boat Trips
Kingswear Castle, Paddle Steamer, The Historic Dockyard, Chatham, ME4 4TQ
☎ 01634 827648
Sail back in time on the Medway. Also sails from Rochester Pier.

Landmark Visitors Guide: Kent; ISBN: 9781843063797; £9.99

Salisbury, Wiltshire

Getting There

By Road

From the east, M3, J8, A303/A338; from west A303/A36; from north, Oxford on A34/A303 then A338.

By Rail & Bus

Few direct rail links and you may have to change trains on the way.

There are coach/bus companies offering a service to Salisbury.

Background Briefing

Salisbury is beautifully situated where the rivers Nadder and Bourne flow into the Avon. Medieval streets have historic buildings at every turn from Tudor half-timbered town houses to Victorian villas. There are Queen Ann Houses and Georgian mansions, historic inns, ancient almshouses, a 17th century Joiners' Hall and an 18th century Guildhall. The jewel in Salisbury's crown is the magnificent early English Gothic cathedral with its graceful spire, the tallest in England. Climb the 332 steps to the top of the tower for breathtaking views over the city.

Explore the impressive Cathedral Close, the largest in the country and a haven of peace and tranquillity, where there are many grand houses, some now used as museums. Mompesson House, an elegant Queen Anne mansion, has a wonderful oak staircase and intricate plasterwork and a fine collection of Turnball drinking glasses. This NT property was used as a film location for Sense and Sensibility in 1995.

Visit the Salisbury & South Wiltshire Museum in the King's House or The Rifles (Berkshire and Wiltshire) Museum in The Wardrobe. In the Medieval Hall you can watch 'Discover Salisbury', an entertaining film about Salisburys history, or perhaps just walk around the close and be inspired by the diverse and remarkable architecture. Old stone gates in the close wall lead, through enchanting medieval streets, to the Market Square and the Guildhall. Markets have been held in this historic setting since 1219 and now operate on a Tuesday and Saturday.

The 15th century hexagonal Poultry Cross at the junction of Silver Street and Butcher Row is still largely original and has many stone carvings. Hidden behind the mock facade of the Odeon Cinema is an original and typical hall of a 15th century merchant featuring stained glass and a finely crafted ceiling. Salisbury, although steeped in history, is also a modern lively city with cosmopolitan pavement cafes, lively bars and restaurants and a leisure centre. You can visit the theatre or enjoy a flutter at the races. Away from the city centre are several parks and gardens where you can enjoy fabulous riverside walks.

Places to Visit

Salisbury Cathedral

33 The Close, SP1 2EJ
www.salisburycathedral.org.uk
13th century building in an early English Gothic style is surrounded by historic buildings and eight acres of lawns. The elaborate exterior has pointed arches, flying buttresses and a highly decorated west front complete with sixty-seven statues. The spire, the tallest in England, was built in the early 14th century. See the largest cathedral cloisters and the largest and most complete choir stalls in Britain. It includes Europe's oldest working clock, a copy of the Magna Carta, a medieval carved frieze in the Chapter House and the tombs of Edward Seymour and Lady Jane Grey.

Stonehenge (EH)

(10.5 miles/16.5km)
Amesbury, SP4 7DE
☎ 0870 333 1181
www.stonehenge.co.uk
A striking prehistoric monument of unique international importance oriented on the rising and setting sun. An audio tour and refreshments are available.

Fisherton Mill

108 Fisherton Street, SP2 7QY
www.fishertonmill.co.uk
Built in 1880 as a grain mill, now the south of England's largest independent art gallery.

Mompesson House (NT)

The Close, SP1 2EL
☎ 01722 420980
An elegant 18th century house in the Cathedral Close.

Above Top: Stonehenge
Above Bottom: Salisbury Cathedral
Left: St Mary at Salisbury Cathedral

The Medieval Hall

Sarum Street, Michael West Walk, Cathedral Close, SP1 2EY
☎ 01722 412472

The Rifles (Berkshire and Wiltshire) Museum

The Wardrobe, 58 The Close SP1 2EX
☎ 01722 419419

Salisbury & South Wiltshire Museum

The King's House, 65 The Close, SP1 2EN
☎ 01722 332151

Attractions Nearby

Breamore House

(9 miles/14.5km)
Fordingbridge, SP6 2DF
☎ 01725 512 233
www.breamorehouse.com
Magnificent manor house overlooking the Avon Valley on the edge of the New Forest.

Cholderton Charlie's Farm

(11.5 miles/18.5km)
Amesbury Road, Cholderton, SP4 0EW
www.choldertoncharliesfarm.com
Ideal for children with animals, tractor and trailer rides and adventure play area.

Edmondsham House & Gardens

(17.5 miles/28.5km)
Wimborne BH21 5RE
☎ 01725 517 207
A fine Tudor manor house with Georgian additions.

Old Sarum

2 miles north of Salisbury, off A345.
The massive Iron Age hill fort of Old Sarum contains the ruins of a castle, cathedral and bishop's palace.

Rockbourne Roman Villa

(10.5 miles/17km)

Fordingbridge, SP3 3PG
☎ 01725 518541
This Roman villa once stood in the centre of a large farming estate, and is the largest known villa in the area. Its history spans the period from the Iron Age to the 5th century AD.

Wilton House

(3.5 miles/5.5km)
Wilton SP2 0BJ
☎ 01722 746714
www.wiltonhouse.co.uk

Events

Salisbury's 28th Beerex

Salisbury Festival

Hotels & Dining

Try the local Tourist Information Centre, see Essential Contacts for details.

Something Special

Grasmere House Hotel

70 Harnham Road, SP2 8JN
☎ 01722 338388
www.grasmerehotel.com
This hotel, in a beautiful riverside setting, has elegantly decorated rooms; the Conservatory Restaurant, also known as "The Bistro on the River", has spectacular views over Grasmere's gardens down to the rivers Nadder and Avon and across the water meadows to Salisbury Cathedral.

Howard's House

(8 miles/13km)
Teffont Evias, SP3 5RJ
☎ 01772 716392
www.howardshousehotel.co.uk
Country house hotel and restaurant set in two acres of glorious gardens in a beautiful Wiltshire village.

Mercure White Hart

St John Street, SP1 2SD
☎ 01722 327476
www.mercure.com
This 17th century three star hotel

with sixty-eight en suite rooms stands in the centre of Salisbury overlooking the famous cathedral.

Landmark Trust

The Wardrobe, Cathedral Close
Top floor above Regimental Museum. Sleeps four.

Milford Hall Hotel

206 Castle Street, SP1 3TE
☎ 01722 417 411
www.milfordhallhotel.com
Within easy walking distance of the city with meals served in a smart brasserie restaurant.

One Minster Street Restaurant

Minster Street, SP1 1TB
☎ 01722 411 313
www.haunchofvenison.uk.com

The Lemon Tree

92 Crane Street, SP1 2QD
☎ 01722 333471
www.thelemontreesalisbury.co.uk
In the heart of the historic city near to the cathedral, serving natural produce, freshly cooked to order.

Essential Contacts

Tourist Information Centre

Fish Row SP1 1EJ
☎ 01722 334956

Salisbury Arts Centre

Bedwin Street, nr Market Square, SP1 3UT
☎ 01722 321744

Salisbury City Guides

☎ 01722 320349
www.salisburycityguides.co.uk
A variety of themed walks are available.

Salisbury Playhouse

Malthouse Lane, SP2 7RA
☎ 01722 320333

Salisbury Racecourse

Netherhampton SP2 8PN
☎ 01722 326461

Skipton, Yorkshire

Getting There

By Road

From the west 12 miles from the end of the M65, which terminates at Colne; from the south via Leeds and the M1 or from the north via the A1 and Ripon.

By Rail & Bus

There are services to Skipton Rail Station from around the country.

You can travel to Skipton by coach/bus although you may have to make several changes.

Background Briefing

Skipton is an attractive historic market town, having been granted its market rights by King John in 1204. Today this thriving town still holds markets on the High Street four days a week. The markets and the many independent specialist shops together with branches of quality chains and a couple of department stores make shopping in Skipton a must. The town has cobbled streets, fascinating ginnels (alleyways), historic coaching inns and yards together with a medieval castle. Wander round the streets and alleyways or join one of the guided tours that begin outside the Tourist Information Centre. Skipton's Historic 'Gateway' Guided Walk is a non-strenuous walk, lasting about one and a half hours, which takes the visitor round the historic heart of the town.

The Skipton Millennium Walk Guided Tour includes the historic town but also takes you to areas off the beaten track such as 'Black Walk' and 'The Wilderness'. The Leeds and Liverpool canal passes right through the centre of the town and the canal basin is an ideal place to simply sit and watch the colourful narrowboats go by. Once a year, the canal basin is the venue for the Skipton Waterway Festival, the largest annual meeting of canal boats in the north of England.

Why not take a boat trip or walk along the network of towpaths by the canal. Every year the town celebrates its farming traditions with a 'Sheep Day'; after all, the meaning of Skipton is 'sheeptown'. Sheep Day is held in July on the setts in the High Street where sheep are sheared and ducks are herded. Skipton prides itself on being 'The Gateway to the Dales' and the many attractions and scenic delights of the Yorkshire Dales National Park are just a short distance away. Nearby is the historic station at Embsay where you can travel by steam locomotive through glorious countryside to Bolton Abbey.

Places to Visit

Bolton Abbey Estate

Bolton Abbey, BD23 6EX
☎ 01756 718000

Bolton Priory was built by the Augustinian Canons and ruined by Henry VIII. This beautiful, well-kept country estate with its 12th century priory ruins has over eighty miles of riverside, woodland and moorland paths, picnic areas, tearooms and restaurants, gift shops and fabulous scenery.

Skipton Castle

Skipton, BD23 1AQ
☎ 01756 792442
www.skiptoncastle.co.uk
Skipton Castle is one of the best-preserved complete medieval castles in the country. The 11th century castle standing impressively at the top of the town's main street was involved in the Wars of the Roses and was a Royalist stronghold during the Civil War. Visitors can explore the dungeon, view the banqueting hall, kitchen, bed-chamber and privy and can climb to

Canal boats moored in Skipton

the top of the watchtower. Inside the castle there is a tranquil Tudor courtyard.

Holy Trinity Church

High Street, BD23 1NJ
☎ 01756 700773
www.holytrinityskipton.co.uk
This ancient medieval church has a 12th century foundation but has architecture dating mainly from the 14th and 15th centuries. The church has a bossed 15th century roof a fine rood screen and is resplendent with banners and coats of arms.

The Craven Museum

Town Hall, High Street,
BD23 1AH
☎ 01756 706407
A great place to explore the history of Skipton and the Craven Dales.

Attractions Nearby

Embsay & Bolton Abbey Steam Railway

(5 miles/8km)
Bolton Abbey Station, BD23 6AF
☎ 01756 710614
www.embsayboltonabbeyrailway.org.uk
Board a steam train at historic Embsay station, built in 1888, and journey through the picturesque Yorkshire Dales scenery to the new award-winning station at Bolton Abbey. Alight from the train and enjoy a pleasant one and a half mile walk to the ruins of the 12th

century priory.

Brontë Parsonage Museum
(13 miles/22km)
Church Street, Haworth, Keighley, BD22 8DR
☎ 01535 642323
www.bronte.org.uk
Get a new view of the story of the Brontë family and an opportunity to see behind the scenes.

Cliffe Castle Museum
(7 miles/11km)
Spring Gardens Lane, Keighley, BD20 6LH
☎ 01535 618 231
Cliffe Castle stands in attractive hillside grounds with greenhouses and garden centre, aviaries and a children's play area.

East Riddlesden Hall (NT)
(10 miles/16km)
Bradford Road, Keighley, BD20 5EL
☎ 01535 607 075
17th century West Riding manor house with formal and wild gardens, duck pond and grounds.

Grassington Village in Wharfedale
(8 miles/13km)
www.grassington.net
Picturesque village with cobbled streets, interesting shops, the Dales Visitor Centre and the Upper Wharfedale Museum.

Keighley & Worth Valley Railway
(13 miles/21km)
The Railway Station, Haworth, Keighley, BD22 8NJ
☎ 01535 645214
Famous as the setting for The Railway Children with beautifully preserved stations complete with period enamel signs and flower baskets.

Parcevall Hall Gardens
(12 miles/19km)
Skyreholme, Skipton, BD23 6DE
☎ 01756 720311
www.parcevallhallgardens.co.uk
The gardens are situated in the Yorkshire Dales National Park.

Saltaire
(15 miles/24km)
www.saltairevillage.info
Saltaire was a complete 'model' industrial village for Sir Titus Salt's workers. In December 2001, Saltaire was designated a World Heritage Site by Unesco.

Hotels & Dining
Try the local Tourist Information Centre, see Essential Contacts for details.

Something Special

The Devonshire Arms Country House Hotel & Spa
Bolton Abbey, BD23 6AJ
☎ 01756 718142
www.devonshireclub.co.uk
In a delightful setting on the Bolton Abbey Estate in the Yorkshire Dales, this historic country estate hotel is surrounded by open parkland stretching down to the River Wharfe. The health spa facilities include jacuzzi, steam room, sauna, cold plunge pool, gym, poolside relaxation lounge, all-weather tennis court and beauty therapy rooms.

Rendezvous @ Skipton
Keighley Road, BD23 2TA
☎ 01756 700100
Delightful waterside location, complete with leisure centre offering swimming pool, steam, sauna, whirlpool spa, gym and beauty treatment rooms.

Landmark Trust
Beamsley Hospital, nr Skipton
A round almshouse, built in 1593. Sleeps five.

Nosh Brasserie and Bar
1 Devonshire Place, Skipton,

Top – Bottom: Shoppers in Skipton; Rippon Spa Garden; Skipton Canal

BD3 2LR
☎ 01756 700060
Modern brasserie style food, tapas bites, light lunches, evening á la carte and Sunday lunch.

Canalside
Waterside Court, Coach Street, BD23 1LH
☎ 01756 795678
On the canal basin and a perfect place to watch the world go by. Carvery and a la carte menu.

Events
Medieval Yuletide Festival

Sheep Day

Waterway Festival

Essential Contacts

Tourist Information Centre
35 Coach Street, BD23 1LQ
☎ 01756 792809
www.skiptononline.co.uk

Pennine Cruisers
19 Coach Street, BD23 1LH
☎ 01756 795478
www.penninecruisers.com

Landmark Publishing is grateful to Yorkshire Dales & Harrogate Tourism Partnership for the photographs on page 89. www.yorkshiredales.org

Stamford, Lincolnshire

Getting There

By Road
Stamford is just off the A1.

By Rail & Bus
There are rail services into Stamford Railway Station from around the country.

There are national coach/bus services into Stamford from around the country although it may involve changes to complete the journey.

Background Briefing
Stamford is one of the finest stone towns in England, owing its prosperity to the woollen industry and to its position on the stagecoach route between London and York. The town retains part of its medieval street pattern and can easily be explored on foot. Walk through quaint cobbled streets and narrow passageways and delight in the beautiful mellowed stone buildings, which include Georgian mansions, Queen Ann houses, ancient coaching inns and medieval churches. Rich treasures can be discovered around every corner, from 15th century almshouses, to an 18th century theatre where Keane and Sheridan once performed.

Add to that a ruined priory, an old Town Hall and wonderful water meadows perfect for strolling along the banks of the River Welland; it is not surprising that Stamford has been the setting for many period dramas including Middlemarch and Pride and Prejudice.

One of the largest and finest street markets in England is held in Broad Street on Fridays and a Farmers' Market is held fortnightly. The pedestrianised town centre has a wide range of specialist shops including antiques, crafts, books and gifts together with major high-street retailers. There are numerous places to eat, whether your choice is a restaurant in an historic inn, a cafe or a tearoom; there is something for everyone. While in town visit the museum and the former Victorian steam-operated brewery, walk along the water meadows or take a trip on a punt along the river. Town Trail.

Nearby are pleasant walks through beautiful countryside and delightful limestone villages. You can fish, sail and birdwatch at Rutland Water and of course visit the magnificent Burghley House with its deer park and sculpture garden.

Places to Visit

Burghley House
Barnack Road, PE9 3JY
☎ 01780 752451
www.burghley.co.uk
Completed by William Cecil, Lord Burghley in 1587 and is a family home for his descendants to this day. It is the largest and greatest house of the first Elizabethan age where visitors can access eighteen staterooms filled with paintings, furniture and fine art. It is set in a fabulous deer park, landscaped by Capability Brown, enjoy walks around the grounds and admire the sculpture garden. The House featured as Rosings, the home of Lady Catherine de Bourgh, in the film of Pride and Prejudice.

All Saints Brewery
All Saints Street, PE9 2PA
☎ 01780 752186
Restored Victorian steam-operated brewery, with award-winning fruit beers. It has a coffee lounge, restaurant and brewery shop.

Browne's Hospital
Broad Street
☎ 01780 763153
Almshouse built in 1474 with original furniture and stained glass.

St John's Church
High Street
An outstanding Perpendicular church with a fine collection of 15th century winged angels on the ceiling of the nave. The font is 14th century and the altar frontal dates from 1718.

St Martin's Church
The only medieval church to survive outside the town walls has splendid tombs to the Cecil family of Burghley House.

Stamford Arts Centre
27 St Mary's Street, PE9 2DL
☎ 01780 763203
www.stamfordartscentre.com
Drama, cinema, dance, music, theatre workshops and exhibitions.

Stamford Museum
Broad Street, PE9 1PJ
☎ 01780 766317
Sets out the history and archaeology of the town from its earliest times to today.

Attractions Nearby

Barnsdale Gardens
(9 miles/14.5km)
The Avenue, Exton, Oakham
LE15 8AH
☎ 01572 813 200
www.barnsdalegardens.co.uk
Designed by the late Geoff Hamilton, comprising thirty-seven individual gardens and features that blend together into an eight acre garden.

Oakham Castle
(9 miles/14.5km)
Market Place, Oakham,
LE15 6DX
☎ 01572 758440
A fine example of late 12th century domestic architecture

Rutland County Museum
(9 miles/14.5km)
Catmose Street, Oakham,

LE15 6HW
☎ 01572 758440

Elton Hall
(10.5 miles/17km)
Near Peterborough, PE8 6SH
☎ 01832 280468
www.eltonhall.com
Romantic hall surrounded by stunning gardens.

Flag Fen Bronze Age Centre
(18.5 miles/30km)
The Droveway, Northey Road, Peterborough, PE6 7QJ
☎ 01733 313414
www.flagfen.com

Grimsthorpe Castle Park & Gardens
(13 miles/20.5km)
Bourne, PE10 0LY
☎ 01778 591205
www.grimsthorpe.co.uk

Nene Valley Railway
(8.5 miles/13.5km)
Wansford Station, Stibbington, PE8 6LR
www.nvr.org.uk

Peterborough Cathedral
(15 miles/25.5km)
Minster Precincts PE1 1XS
☎ 01733 355300
www.peterborough-cathedral.org.uk

The Prebendal Manor House
(8.5 miles/14km)
Nassington, nr Peterborough, PE8 6QG
☎ 01780 782575
www.prebendal-manor.co.uk

Southwick Hall
(14.5 miles/23km)
Southwick, PE8 5BL
☎ 01832 274 064
www.southwickhall.co.uk

Events
Burghley Horse Trials

Stamford Antiques Fair

Stamford Car Show

Stamford Riverside Music Festival

Stamford Shakespeare Festival

Hotels & Dining
Try the Tourist Information entre, see Essential Contacts for details.

The George of Stamford
71 St. Martins, PE9 2LB
☎ 01780 750750
www.georgehotelofstamford.com
The George of Stamford is one of England's greatest coaching inns. It retains the charm and atmosphere of its long history yet offers today's guests every modern comfort.

The Garden House Hotel
High Street, St Martins, PE9 2LP
☎ 01780 763 359
www.gardenhousehotel.com
The Garden House Hotel, part of which dates back to 1796, has been transformed into a beautiful twenty room hotel, retaining both charm and comfort.

Hambleton Hall
(12 miles/ 19km)
Hambleton, Oakham LE15 8TH
☎ 01572 756 991
www.hambletonhall.com
One of Britain's finest country house hotels in a wonderful lakeside setting with fine dining in an award-winning restaurant, a haven for gourmets and wine lovers.

Something Special

Finnan's Brasserie
8–9 St Paul's Street, PE9 2BE
☎ 01780 752505
www.finnansbrasserie.co.uk
Serves fabulous European food.

The Collyweston Slater
(4 miles/6km)
87–89 Main Road, Collyweston, PE9 3PQ
☎ 01780 444 288

Top - Bottom: View from All Saints' spire; Burghley House; Stamford; The George Hotel

Modern British cuisine in a picturesque village.

Essential Contacts

Tourist Information Centre
Stamford Arts Centre, 27 St Mary's Street, PE9 1PJ
☎ 01780 755611

Guided Walks
Jill Collinge
☎ 01780 410780

Spires Chauffeured Punting
River Welland, Town Bridge, Stamford
☎ 01780 755611

Stamford Shakespeare Company
Tolethorpe Hall
☎ 01780 756133
www.stamfordshakespeare.co.uk

Landmark Publishing gratefully acknowledge Lincolnshire Tourism Ltd for the use of the images on pages 91.
www.visitlincolnshire.com

Getting There

By Road

M40 south and north, J15, A46/A3400; from the west, M5 to A422 then A46 (slow but scenic).

By Rail & Bus

There are train services to Stratford-upon-Avon Rail Station.

There are bus/coach services to Stratford Riverside bus station although there are few direct routes.

Background Briefing

Famous as the birthplace of William Shakespeare. It is a delightful place to visit; its wide streets are lined with many historically interesting buildings with many dating from the early 16th century. The town has numerous attractions associated with William Shakespeare and his family. Visit the house where he was born in 1564, or Ann Hathaway's Cottage where he courted the girl who became his wife. Don't miss 'Shakespearience' where groundbreaking technology is used to tell the story of the bard's life and works. Children will enjoy the Brass Rubbing Centre down by the river, and the Butterfly Farm where there are hundreds of the world's most spectacular butterflies and where you can choose to get up close and personal with some dangerous spiders in Arachnoland.

However, Stratford is still an important market centre and a Farmers' Market is held in Rother Street on the first and third Saturdays of every month. A walk around the old town is a rewarding experience and you can do it yourself or join one of the popular guided walking tours. Alternatively enjoy the views on a horse-drawn trip or take a tour on an open-top bus as you are taken around the sights. There are also boat trips along the tranquil River Avon.

Throughout the year a varied programme of events and activities takes place, from theatrical productions to river racing, so there is something for everyone. Stratford is well known for the Royal Shakespeare Company, which is currently staging productions at the Courtyard Theatre and the Civic Hall as the other theatres are being redeveloped. Stratford is the perfect place for a short break not only for the town itself but also as a base to explore the Cotswolds and surrounding countryside.

Places to Visit

Ann Hathaway's Cottage

Cottage Lane, Shottery, CV37 9HH

☎ 01789 204016

A picturesque substantial Elizabethan farmhouse, with beautiful award-winning gardens, home of William Shakespeare's wife and just a mile west of Stratford.

Mary Arden's House

Station Road, Wilmcote, CV37 9UN

☎ 01789 204016

The home of Shakespeare's grandparents and childhood home of Shakespeare's mother, Mary Arden. Discover the Elizabethan way of life and interact with the daily domestic routine of a working farm.

Shakespearience

Waterside, CV37 6BA

☎ 01789 290111

www.shakespearience.co.uk

A theatrical spectacular with gusts of wind, claps of thunder and flashes of lightning. Thrilling special effects help to bring Shakespeare to life.

Shakespeare's Birthplace

Henley Street, CV37 6QW

☎ 01789 204016

This is the house where Shakespeare was born and where he spent the first years of his marriage with his new wife.

Brass Rubbing Centre

Royal Shakespeare Theatre, Summer House, Avon Bank Gardens, Southern Lane, CV37 6XP

☎ 01789 297671

www.stratfordbrassrubbing.co.uk

The Butterfly Farm

Swan's Nest Lane, CV37 7LS

☎ 01789 299288

www.butterflyfarm.co.uk

The Creaky Cauldron

21 Henley Street, CV37 6QW

☎ 01789 290969

www.creakycauldron.org

Situated over the first and second floors this Museum of Witchcraft and Wizardology, in one of the most haunted buildings in the country, is Stratford's most magical and unusual tourist attraction.

The Falstaffs Experience

Sheep Street, CV37 6EE

☎ 0870 3502770

www.falstaffexperience.co.uk

Harvard House

26 High Street, CV37 6AU

☎ 01789 204016

An elegant example of an Elizabethan town house.

Holy Trinity Church

Southern Lane, CV37 6BH

☎ 01789 266316

www.stratford-upon-avon.org

This is one of England's most beautiful parish churches where you can visit Shakespeare's and Ann Hathaway's graves.

Hall's Croft

Old Town, CV37 6BG

☎ 01789 204016

17th century home of Shakespeare's eldest daughter, Susanna, and her husband Dr John Hall, an eminent physician.

Nash's House & New Place

Chapel Street, CV37 6EP

☎ 01789 292325
Discover the tragic history of New Place, William Shakespeare's final retirement home.

Attractions Nearby

Charlecote Park (NT)
(4.5 miles/7km)
Warwick, CV35 9ER
☎ 01789 470277
A superb Tudor house with landscaped deer park.

Warwick Castle
Warwick CV34 4QU
☎ 0870 442 2000
www.warwick-castle.co.uk
A wonderful medieval experience.

Events
Beer Festival
Digital Film Festival
International Literary Festival
Music Festival

Hotels & Dining
Try the local Tourist Information Centre, see Essential Contacts for details.

Something Special

Macdonald Alveston Manor
Off Banbury Road, CV37 7HP
☎ 0844 879 9138
www.alvestonhotel.co.uk
Just a few minutes walk away from the town and in a beautiful Tudor building complete with swimming pool, spa and treatment rooms.

Mercure Shakespeare Hotel
Chapel Street, CV37 6ER
☎ 01789 294997
www.mercure.com
The Shakespeare Hotel dates back

to 1637 and is situated in the heart of the town centre.

Landmark Trust
The Bath House, nr Stratford
Elegant bedsit, built at the end of a long gated drive in 1748. Sleeps two.

Countess of Evesham
☎ 07836 769499
www.countessofevesham.mistral.co.uk
A purpose built 70ft restaurant cruiser where you can enjoy a romantic supper along the floodlit banks of the Avon. Fine cuisine with a well-stocked wine list.

Marlowe's Restaurant
18 High Street, CV37 6AU
☎ 01789 204999
Dine in a magnificent Elizabethan dining room.

Essential Contacts

Tourist Information Centre
Bridgefoot, CV37 6GW
☎ 0870 160 7930

Avon Boating Limited
The Boathouse, Swan's Nest Lane, CV37 7LS
☎ 01789 267073
www.avon-boating.co.uk

Bancroft Cruisers
Bridge Foot, CV37 6YR
☎ 01789 269669
www.bancroftcruisers.co.uk

Horse Drawn Trips
☎ 01789 773208
www.kingsmoorcarriages.co.uk

Open-Top Bus Tours
☎ 01789 299123
www.city-sightseeing.co.uk

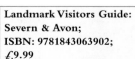

Top – Bottom: Shakespeare's birthplace; Holy Trinity Church; Stratford-upon-Avon canal preston bagot flight of locks; Anne Hathaway's cottage, home of Shakespeare's wife

Stratford Town Walks
☎ 017879 292478
www.stratfordtownwalk.co.uk

Royal Shakespeare Company and Theatres
The Courtyard Theatre, Southern Lane, CV37 6BB
☎ 0844 800 1110
www.rsc.org.uk

Stratford-upon-Avon Racecourse
Luddington Road, CV37 9SE
☎ 01789 267949
www.stratfordracecourse.net

> **Landmark Visitors Guide: Severn & Avon;**
> **ISBN: 9781843063902;**
> **£9.99**
> **Landmark Visitors Guide: Cotswolds & Shakespeare Country;**
> **ISBN: 9781843063247;**
> **£9.99**

Racecourse with new housing and flats

Getting there

By Road

M5, J25, north or south bound.

By Rail & Bus

There are mainline connections from around the country to Taunton.

Background Briefing

Taunton is attractively located between the beautiful Quantock

Taunton Cricket Ground

Top – Bottom: St Mary Magdalene and St James Church; Market House; Shopping in Taunton; Taunton Town Centre; Old municipal buildings

and Blackdown Hills. This town of soaring church towers has lots of interesting architecture including the gabled and half-timbered Tudor House in Fore Street, built in the 1550s, probably the oldest house in town. The nine external chimney pieces on the frontage of Gray's Almshouses in East Street are worth a look as are the buildings around the Market Place, which reflect architectural styles from several eras. Imposing Georgian terraces can be seen in The Crescent at the end of Bath Place; built by Sir Benjamin Hammet in 1801 they are similar to fashionable houses built in London and Bath.

Take the Taunton Heritage Trail to gain a good insight into the history of the town. Attractive brass plaques set in the pavements lead visitors around a circular walk passing many places of interest and revealing fascinating links to Wordsworth, Coleridge and Lord Trenchard (first head of the RAF). Take a look inside the splendid St Mary's Church where the Tudor ceiling of the nave and chancel is adorned with over a hundred gilded angels. Taunton Castle, dating from the 12th century, was once the administrative centre of Taunton Deane manor. Just minutes from the town centre is Somerset County

Cricket Ground where national and international matches are played. Vivery Park in the town centre has a picnic area and is the setting for live outdoor concerts, firework displays and an annual flower show. Goodland Gardens beside the River Tone provide a pleasant place to stroll amid peaceful surroundings.

In addition Taunton has a wide range of shops, malls and stalls offering superb shopping facilities. A farmers' Market is held on the last Thursday of each month where you will find a great variety of local produce, and an Antique Market is open in Silver Street on Mondays.

Places to Visit

Taunton Heritage Trail
Contact Tourist Information
☎ 01823 336344

Hestercombe Gardens
Cheddon Fitzpaine, TA2 8LG
☎ 01823 413923
www.hestercombe.com
Beautiful gardens with woodland walks, formal terraces and breathtaking views. A unique combination of three period gardens; the Georgian (1750–86) The Victorian terrace (1873–78) and the Edwardian garden which was created by Sir Edwin Lutyens.

West Somerset Railway

The Railway Station, Minehead, TA24 5BG

☎ 01643 704996

www.west-somerset-railway.co.uk

Take a trip through Somerset's beautiful countryside along the old Great Western Railway line.

Shakespeare Glass

Riverside Place, TA1 1JJ

☎ 01823 333422

www.shakespeareglass.co.uk

Blown glass and gallery.

The Fun Farm

(2 miles/3.5km)

Nerrols Farm, Priorswood, TA2 8QJ

☎ 01823 270289

www.thefunfarm.org

An indoor and outdoor children's adventure play centre.

Somerset Cricket Museum

7 Priory Avenue, TA1 1XX

☎ 01823 275893

www.somersetcountycc.premiumtv.co.uk

Cricketing memorabilia dating back to the foundation of the Somerset County Cricket Club in 1875, housed in an historic barn.

Taunton Racecourse

(2 miles/3.5km)

Orchard, Portman, Taunton, TA3 7BL

☎ 01823 337172

www.tauntonracecourse.co.uk

Attractions Nearby

Bishops Lydeard Mill

(4miles/6.5km)

The Mill House

Mill Lane, Bishops Lydeard, nr Taunton, TA4 3LN

☎ 01823 432151

www.bishopslydeardmill.co.uk

Sheppy's Cider Farm

(4 miles/6.5km)

Bradford on Tone, nr Taunton, TA4 1ER

☎ 01823 461233

www.sheppyscider.com

Discover how cider is made and savour the marvellous aroma of aged oak vats and cider in the cellars. Try a little tasting, visit the museum and shop or relax in the picnic area.

Willow and Wetlands Visitor Centre

(9.5 miles/15km)

Meare Green Court, Stoke St Gregory, nr Taunton, TA3 6HY

☎ 01823 490249

www.englishwillowbaskets.co.uk

Guided tours of willow industry and basket making available here.

RSPB West Sedgemoor

(12 miles/19km)

www.rspb.org.uk

☎ 01458 252805

Hotels & Dining

Try the local Tourist Information Centre for details of local hotels and B&Bs.

The Library, Paul Street, TA1 3XZ

Accommodation Booking Line

☎ 01823 336344

email: tauntontic@tauntondeane.gov.uk

Something Special

Cedar Falls Health Spa

Bishops Lydeard, Taunton, TA4 3HR

☎ 01823 433233

www.cedarfallssw.co.uk

Health spa resort set in fourty-four acres of wooded landscape.

The Mount Somerset

Lower Henlade, TA3 5NB

☎ 01823 442500

www.mountsomersethotel.co.uk

An elegant Regency country house hotel cradled by both the Quantocks and the Blackdown Hills.

Landmark Trust

The Priests House, Holcombe Rogus

Built around 1500, sleeps five.

Robin Hood's Hut

Haswell House, Goathurst

18th century folly with fine views, sleeps two.

www.landmarktrust.co.uk

The Restaurant at The Castle Hotel

Castle Green, TA1 1NF

☎ 01823 272671

www.the-castle-hotel.com

Fine dining in spectacular surroundings.

Essential Contacts

The Brewhouse Theatre and Arts Centre

Coal Orchard, Taunton, TA1 1JL

☎ 01823 28244

www.thebrewhouse.net

Top: Vivary Park; Bottom: Vivary

Landmark Publishing gratefully acknowledges Somerset Tourism Partnership www.visitsomerset.co.uk for the use of the images on pages 94 & 95.

Landmark Visitors Guide: Somerset;
ISBN: 9781843063285;
£9.99

Truro, Cornwall

Above: The Eden Project; **Right:** St Just-in-Roseland church

Getting There

By Road

M5 then A30/A39.

By Train

All trains to Cornwall from England run through Plymouth. The Cornish mainline to Penzance then travels through Liskeard, Bodmin, St. Austell and Truro.

There are coach/bus services to the main bus station in Truro from around the country.

Background Briefing

Truro was once an important river port and a rich stannary town, a place where tin was assayed and stamped. The town today is full of character and charm with picturesque streets lined with Georgian and Victorian architecture. Elegant town houses of wealthy merchants can still be seen in Princes Street. Lemon Street is thought to be one of the best-preserved Georgian streets in England and the late Georgian crescent, Walsingham Place, is sometimes described as 'the jewel in Truro's crown'.

Truro was popular with the local gentry in the 18th century who attended balls in the Assembly Rooms and enjoyed entertainment at the theatre. Other architectural gems include the Italianate City Hall, the Plaza Cinema with its 1930s facade, the Royal Cornwall Museum and of course the splendid Gothic Revival cathedral.

The Hall for Cornwall in Back Quay is Cornwall's premier entertainment venue. Truro is well known as the shopping capital of Cornwall and many pleasurable hours can be spent browsing shops in the cobbled streets and the narrow passageways known as opes. Lemon Quay has a large indoor market, a Farmers Market on Wednesdays and Saturdays and regular continental markets. Pleasant walks along the river lead to Malpas and St Clements and river trips leave Truro town quay to Falmouth and St Mawes. Truro makes an ideal base for exploring Cornwall with excellent access to the road network, and it is in easy reach of the north and south coast and the beautiful Roseland Peninsular.

Places to Visit

Royal Cornwall Museum

River Street TR1 2SJ
☎ 01872 272205
www.royalcornwallmuseum.org.uk

Cornwall's oldest and most prestigious museum displaying Cornish history and famed for its internationally important collections. The Fine and Decorative Arts gallery includes a collection of Newlyn School paintings.

Truro Cathedral

High Cross, TR1 2AF
www.trurocathedral.org.uk

The cathedral with its three soaring towers and high vaulted nave was completed in 1910 and was the first to be built in Britain since St Paul's.

Attractions Nearby

St Mawes Castle (EH)

(10.5 miles/17km)
Castle Drive, St Mawes TR2 5DE
☎ 01326 270526

A Tudor coastal fortress with three huge circular bastions.

Trelissick Garden (NT)

(5 miles/8km)
Feock, TR3 6QL
☎ 01872 862090

Catch the ferry from Truro and alight at this beautiful waterside garden (above the King Harry Ferry). Follow trails meandering through woodland or walk the riverside path. Restaurant and shop.

Bandstand, Victoria Gardens

The Church
St Just-in-Roseland, TR2 5JD
Set at the side of Carrick Roads (the sea, near King Harry Ferry).
One of the most tranquil places in the country. The churchyard is a botanical garden with stream, pools etc.

Bosvigo Gardens
(1 mile/1.5km)
Bosvigo Lane, TR1 3NH
☎ 01872 275774
www.bosvigo.com

Cornish Cyder Farm
(5.5 miles/8.5km)
Penhallow, TR4 9LW
☎ 01872 573356
www.thecornishcyderfarm.co.uk

Trewithen House & Gardens
(7.5 miles/12km)
Grampound Road, nr Truro, TR2 4DD
☎ 01726 883647
www.trewithengardens.co.uk

National Maritime Museum Cornwall
(11 miles/18km)
Discovery Quay, Falmouth, TR11 3QY
www.nmmc.co.uk

Pendennis Castle (EH)
(12 miles/19km)
Falmouth, TR11 4LP
☎ 01326 316594

The Eden Project
(20 miles/32km)
Bodleva, PL24 2SG
☎ 01726 811911

www.edenproject.com
Huge biomes, the largest conservatories in the world, emulate tropical and Mediterranean environments. Outside plants from Chile, the Himalayas, Asia and Australia thrive in Cornwall's mild climate.

Events
The Cornwall Food and Drink Festival

Truro Carnival

Truro City of Lights

Hotels & Dining
Try the local Tourist Information Centre, see Essential Contacts for details.

Something Special
The Alverton Manor Hotel
Tregolls Road, TR1 1ZQ
☎ 01872 276 633
www.alvertonmanor.co.uk
Country house hotel within walking distance of Truro's amenities. Elegant atmosphere in a beautiful building.

Nare Hotel
Carne Beach, Veryan-in-Roseland, TR2 5PF
☎ 01872 501111
www.thenare.com
Overlooking beautiful Carne beach on the Roseland Peninsula, the Nare is Cornwall's highest rated hotel.

Tabb's Restaurant
85 Kenwyn Street, TR1 3BZ
☎ 01872 262110
Sophisticated dining and mouth-watering meals.

Stingi Lulu's
Royal Cornwall Museum, River Street, TR1 2SJ
☎ 01872 262300
www.stingilulus.com
A unique dining experience based on seafood, shellfish, meat and

poultry infused with Japanese Thai and Indonesian flavours.

Essential Contacts
Tourist Information Office
The Municipal Buildings, Boscawen Street, TR1 2NE
☎ 01872 274555

Boat Trips
Town Quay
☎ 01326 313234

Hall for Cornwall
Back Quay, TR12LL
☎ 01872 262466
www.hallforcornwall.co.uk
A large scale theatre in the centre of Truro which presents a wide range of performances including drama, dance, music and comedy.

King Harry Ferry
Feock, TR3 6QJ
☎ 01872 862312

Newmans Cruises
Tolverne, Philleigh, Truro, TR2 5NG
☎ 01872 580309

National Maritime Museum

Pendennis Castle

Landmark Visitors Guide: Cornwall & the Isles of Scilly;
ISBN: 9781843063711;
£9.99

Wells, Somerset

Getting There

By Road

M5 J 23, A39 to Glastonbury and Wells.

By Rail & Bus

The nearest mainline station is Bridgewater some thirty miles away.

It is possible to travel to Wells by coach and bus although there are no direct routes.

Background Briefing

Wells is a delightful city; one of England's smallest and dominated by its awe-inspiring cathedral. Located in rolling countryside at the foot of the Mendip Hills, it is an unspoilt market town still holding weekly markets on Saturdays and Wednesdays. The city retains a medieval atmosphere and provides a wealth of historical interest and beautiful architecture. The cobble-stoned Vicar's Close, near the cathedral has 14th century houses with striking chimneys. It is thought to be the oldest planned street in Europe. The Bishop's Palace at Wells is probably the most perfect and complete surviving example of a medieval bishop's palace. It is surrounded by a moat where mute swans glide and fish swim lazily in the tranquil waters. Parts of the palace are open to the public but the 15th century north wing, the private residence of the Bishop of Bath and Wells, is out of bounds.

The cathedral is one of the best surviving examples of medieval English Gothic style and dates back to 1180. Its spectacular west front looks over the Cathedral Green and still has a great many medieval figures depicting, among others, saints, angels, kings and bishops. Although now glowing softly in golden limestone the statues were originally painted with brightly coloured pigments and must have been a stunning sight. The Bishop's Barn, in Silver Street, is a medieval tithe barn once used by the Bishop to store harvest produce paid to him by way of tax. Several quaint streets, full of independent shops, surround the historic city centre and several 15th century buildings, built by Bishop Bekynton, stand nearby.

An enjoyable scenic walk can be taken following a self-guided trail available from the Tourist Information Office located in the Georgian Town Hall. Wells is perfectly placed to explore the beautiful Somerset countryside with its delightful villages, and the wetlands of the Somerset levels to the south with marshes and rhynes vibrant with bird life.

Places to Visit

The Cathedral Church of St Andrew

Wells Cathedral was built in the Early English Gothic Style and has a superb interior as well as the magnificent west front externally. Unique scissor arches support the nave, which together with the octagonal Chapter House has a fan-vaulted ceiling. The Chapter House has some of the best-preserved medieval glass in the entire country and an intricate star-vault. Other notable features include carved misericords under the stall in the choir, fine capitols and corbels in the nave and transepts, and a remarkable astronomical clock. The clock has jousting knights and a figure called 'Jack Blandiver', a wooden quarter jack who kicks the quarter hours with his heels.

The Bishop's Palace

This fortified and moated medieval palace, described by Nicholas Pevsner as '...the most memorable of all Bishop's Palaces in England', dates from the early 13th century and has been the home of the Bishops of Bath and Wells for over 800 years. Visitors can see the Bishop's private Chapel, the ruined Great Hall and the Gatehouse complete with portcullis and drawbridge. Good views can be seen from the Rampart Walk while the peaceful and tranquil gardens provide pleasant walks.

Wells and Mendip Museum

8 Cathedral Green, BA5 2UE
☎ 01749 673477
www.wellsmuseum.org.uk
Displays the past and present life of Wells and the Mendip area.

St. Cuthbert's Church

Wells
This church, built in fine Somerset stone, is designed on an impressive scale. It has a lovelt-tower and an intricately carved roof decorated with angels, rosettes and shields.

Milton Lodge Gardens

Old Bristol Road, BA5 3AQ
☎ 01749 672168
www.miltonlodgegardens.co.uk
Glorious gardens on the slopes of the Mendip Hills with panoramic views over Wells.

Attractions Nearby

Burcott Mill

(2 miles/3.5km)
Wookey, nr Wells, BA5 1NJ
☎ 01749 673118
www.burcottmill.com
Water-powered working flour-mill with machinery dating from around 1864.

Cheddar Caves and Gorge

(9 miles/14.5km)
Cheddar, BS27 3QF
☎ 01934 742343
www.cheddarcaves.com

Glastonbury

(6 miles/10km)

Left: Vicar's Close; Above Left: A view from the top of the Mendip Hills; Above Right: Wells Cathedral; Below Left: Interior of Wells Cathedral; Below Right: Entrance to Bishop's Palace

Historic town, with majestic Abbey grounds, associated with the legend of King Arthur. There are splendid views from the top of the Tor and lots of unusual and interesting shops.

Wookey Hole Caves and Papermill

(2 miles/3.5km)
Nr Wells, BA5 1BB
☎ 01749 672243
Spectacular underground caverns, 19th century papermill and attractions for all the family.

Hotels & Dining

Try the local Tourist Information Centre, see Essential Contacts for details.

Something Special

Manor Farm Bed and Breakfast

Old Frome Road, East Horrington
BA5 3DP
☎ 01749 679832
An absolutely stunning Grade II listed home dating back to the 14th century and containing a wealth

of exciting and unusual original period features.

Manor Farm is located high up on the Mendip Hills. It is in the centre of East Horrington village and just two miles from the cathedral city of Wells.

Millers at Glencote House

Glencote Lane, Wookey Hole,
Wells, BA5 1BH
☎ 01749 677160
www.glencotehouse.co.uk
A country house hotel in a Victorian mansion built in grand Jacobean style with sumptuous interiors and wonderful facilities including sauna and plunge pool.

Landmark Trust

The Parish House, Baltonsborough (eight miles south of Wells)
Sleeps four.

The Old Hall

Croscombe
The great hall of a manor house, built around 1420. Sleeps five.

Bekynton Brasserie

23 Market Place, BA5 2RF
☎ 01749 675993

Fountain Inn & Boxers Restaurant

1 St Thomas Street BA5 2UU
☎ 01749 672317
www.thefountaininn.co.uk

Ritchers Restaurant

5 Sadler Street
☎ 01749 679085

Essential Contacts

Tourist Information Centre

Town Hall, Market Place,
BA5 2RB
☎ 01749 672552

Wells Cathedral

Cathedral Green, Wells, BA5 2UE
www.wellscathedral.org.uk

The Bishop's Palace

Wells
☎ 01749 678691
www.bishopspalacewells.co.uk

Landmark Visitors Guide: Somerset; ISBN: 9781843063285; £9.99

Top – Bottom: Whitby harbour; Whitby steps; Gracestones overlooking the bay

Getting There

By Road

A169 from York; A171 from Middlesbrough.

By Rail & Bus

Whitby is on a branch line from Middlesbrough where you can get a connection to most parts of the country.

Some coach/bus companies operate an indirect service, check online for details.

Background Briefing

Whitby is a delightful maritime town and has one of the most picturesque ports in England together with sandy Blue Flag beaches and reputedly the best fish and chips in the country. The town is dominated by the ruined Abbey on the cliff top. The old town retains an old-fashioned air with its market place, chapels, churches, steep yards and fine 18th century houses built by prosperous ship owners.

Although you can get there by road, most people climb the 199 steps to reach the parish church of St Mary with pews carved by local craftsmen. Visitors who are not daunted by the steps might also like to climb to the top of the West Pier Lighthouse and enjoy the best view in town. An easier option is to relax in the peaceful setting of the Crescent Gardens, which also have spectacular coastal views.

Whitby is still a working port and its famous Smokehouse still converts herrings to kippers by this traditional method. Whitby once had a whaling fleet, a fact commemorated by the whale jawbone arch on the West Cliff. Captain Cook is also remembered in the town; a bronze statue of the famous explorer looks out over the sea. Cook was an apprentice here and the house where he lodged with his master is now the Captain Cook Memorial Museum. Another man who is associated with Whitby is Bram Stoker, the author of Dracula; he used parts of Whitby as inspiration for his novel. Whitby's quayside area has attractive harbourside houses and delightful shops where you can buy crafts, antiques, jet jewellery and maritime memorabilia. There is an amazing choice of restaurants serving fish, traditional English food and Continental meals. Not far from town is the North York Moors National Park, ideal for walking or touring.

Places to Visit

Captain Cook Memorial Museum

Grape Lane, YO22 4BA
☎ 01947 601900
www.cookmuseumwhitby.co.uk/
The Museum is in the 17th century house on Whitby's harbour where the young James Cook lodged as an apprentice.

St Mary's Church

At the top of the listed and restored 199 steps is this interesting and unusual church with a Norman tower and 18th century interior. Don't miss the triple decker pulpit, box pews, Elizabethan altar table and the upper gallery.

Whitby Abbey (EH)

The magnificent ruins of the Abbey, founded in the 7th century, are a prominent landmark perched high on a cliff above the town.

Whitby Museum

Pannett Park, YO21 1RE
☎ 01947 602908
www.whitbymuseum.org.uk
An eclectic collection featuring Captain Cook, whalers, shipping, fishing, Whitby jet etc.

Whitby Wizard

West Cliff
☎ 01947 810470
www.whitbywizard.com
An interactive science museum with one hundred hands-on experi-

Top: Whalebone arch; Bottom: Whitby Bay

ments of real science, designed to be used safely and freely by both adults and children.

St Hilda's Anglican Church
Church Square
An imposing neo-Gothic edifice whose impressive interior contains fine examples of stained glass and a bishop's chair, and is richly endowed with carvings in both wood and stone.

The Bram Stoker Dracula Experience
Marine Parade
☎ 01947 601923
www.dracula-in-whitby.com
Bram Stoker's 'Dracula' is brought to life in this walk-through attraction.

Whitby Jet Heritage Centre
123b Church Street, YO22 4DE
www.whitbyjet.net
Original 1867 jet works with working craftsmen.

Fortune's Smokehouse
Buy freshly smoked kippers from Fortune's Smokehouse in the lane at the foot of the Church steps. They close at 4pm.

Attractions Nearby

Cleveland Ironstone Mining Museum
(18 miles/30km)
Skinningrove, Saltburn by the Sea, Cleveland, TS13 4AP
☎ 01287 642877
www.ironstonemuseum.co.uk

Goathland
www.goathland.info
Only nine miles from Whitby and the setting for Yorkshire Television's flagship drama *Heartbeat*.

Scarborough Sea Life and Marine Sanctuary
Scalby Mills, Scarborough, YO12 6RP
☎ 01723 376125

The Dock
Robin Hoods Bay
☎ 01723 383636
The scenic village of Robin Hood's Bay is a magnet for visitors. The main street runs steeply down to the very edge of the rocky shore and there are intriguing alleyways weaving between clustered cottages and houses.

Events
Angling Festival
Captain Cook Festival
Folk Festival
Goth Weekend Festival
Whitby Regatta
Whitby Festival
Enquire at TIC for details of these and other events. ☎ 01723 383637

Hotels & Dining
See Essential Contacts for booking details.

Something Special

Dunsley Hall Country House Hotel
Dunsley, YO21 3TL
☎ 01947 893437
www.dunsleyhall.com
Victorian country house. Dunsley Hall offers traditional comfort and wonderful food against a backdrop of period elegance and modern charm.

Ruswarp Hall Hotel
Ruswarp, YO21 1NH
☎ 01947 602801
www.ruswarphallhotel.co.uk
Within a few minutes walk of the River Esk and just over a mile from Whitby along a country path.

Landmark Trust
The Pigsty, Robin Hoods Bay
Don't be put off this small property and its classical front from the name! Just down the coast from Whitby. Sleeps two.

Top – Bottom: Fortune's Smokery; Whitby Abbey; The harbour

Greens Restaurant & Bistro
13 Bridge Street, YO22 4BG
☎ 01947 600284
Locally sourced food and fish fresh from the quayside.

Trenchers
New Quay Road, YO21 1DH
☎ 01947 603212
www.trenchersrestaurant.co.uk
Traditional fish and chips.

Essential Contacts

Tourist Information Centre
Langborne Road YO21 1YN
☎ 01723 383637
Enquire here for details of:-
Whitby Ghost Walks
In Search of Dracula Walks
Heritage Town Tours

Whitby Coastal Cruisers
☎ 01947 601385
Daily 25-minute boat rides.

Whitby Pavilion Complex
West Cliff
☎ 01947 604855
Whitby Pavilion has wonderful views over the North Sea and is a venue for all types of events.

Winchester Cathedral

Getting There

By Road

Winchester is located just off the M3.

By Rail & Bus

There are train operators offering a service into Winchester Rail Station.

There are coach/bus services into Winchester Bus Station from around the country.

Background Briefing

This enchanting cathedral city, once the capital of the Saxon Kings of Wessex, was described by John Keates as 'the pleasantest town I was ever in', with its Elizabethan and Tudor buildings and a magnificent cathedral which will not disappoint visitors today. Walk around Winchester's narrow, winding streets to discover art galleries, museums, an 18th century water-powered mill and the oldest public school in England. Winchester College has a 14th century Gothic chapel with a wooden fan-vaulted roof while the great hall, the only surviving part of Winchester's Norman castle, has a 13th century round table claimed to be linked to Arthurian Legend.

Wander around the crumbling ruins of Wolvesey Castle, former home of the Bishops of Winchester, then stroll through water meadows to the Hospital of St Cross. This ancient charitable institution has beautiful buildings where there is a medieval hall, Tudor cloisters, a Georgian kitchen and a delightful walled garden to explore. If you ask for the Wayfarers Dole at the porter's gate, you will be given a sip of beer and a morsel of bread. There is also a pleasant walk along the banks of the River Itchen from the castle to High Street.

Jane Austen spent the last six weeks of her life at Winchester; a plaque marks her house in College Street and her grave lies in the north aisle of the cathedral. In the evening why not visit the Theatre Royal or The Screen, a cinema in a converted 19th century chapel. Shopping connoisseurs will be delighted with the appealing range of independent shops in pedestrian-friendly streets, where buskers provide enjoyable entertainment. Additionally the largest Farmers' Market in the UK is held on the second and last Sunday of every month. Winchester is the gateway to the South Downs where picturesque towns and villages, country pubs and stunning scenery await your pleasure.

Places to Visit

Winchester Cathedral

1 The Close, SO23 9LS
☎ 01962 857 200
www.winchester-cathedral.org.uk
This splendid cathedral, with its Romanesque north transept and Perpendicular-style nave, is one of the finest in England. The cathedral has the oldest choir stalls in the country, a beautiful Epiphany chapel, medieval wall paintings and Burne-Jones windows. Don't miss the magnificent 12th century illuminated bible in the library, the Triforum Gallery Museum and Anthony Gormley's bronze in the crypt.

INTECH Science Centre & Planetarium

(2.5 miles/4km)
Telegraph Way, Morn Hill, SO21 1HX
☎ 01962 863 791
www.intech-uk.com
INTECH is a science centre with ninty hands-on exhibits for all the family to enjoy. The UK's largest Planetarium opened at INTECH in March 2008 and is a vast screen and

King Alfred's Statue towers over the spring flowers

digital projection which projects you through the universe. A unique experience with stunning colour and sound.

Mottisfont Abbey & Gardens
(15 miles/24km)
Mottisfont, Romsey, SO51 0LP
☎ 01794 340757
A former 13th century priory set in glorious landscaped grounds where the National Collection of old-fashioned roses can be seen in walled gardens. There are well signposted river and estate walks to be enjoyed.

Other Places to Visit

The Gurkha Museum
Peninsula Barracks, Romsey Road, SO23 8TS
☎ 01962 842832
www.thegurkhamuseum.co.uk

HorsePower, The Museum of The King's Royal Hussars
Peninsula Barracks, Romsey Road, SO23 8TS
☎ 01962 828539
www.army.mod.uk

The Hospital of St Cross
St Cross Road SO23 9SD
☎ 01962 851 375
www.stcrosshospital.co.uk

The Rifles Museum
Peninsula Barracks, Romsey Road SO23 8TS
☎ 01962 828 549
www.army.mod.uk

The Westgate Museum
High Street, SO23 9AP
☎ 01962 869 864
www.winchester.gov.uk

Winchester City Mill (NT)
Bridge Street, SO23 0EJ
☎ 01962 870 057

Winchester City Museum
The Square, SO23 9ES

☎ 01962 863 064
www.winchester.gov.uk
This museum houses Winchester city's original Moot Horn made in the late 12th century.

Attractions Nearby

Broadlands
(10 miles/16m)
Romsey, SO51 9ZD
☎ 01794 505010
www.broadlands.net
Open for guided tours in summer months.

Jane Austen's House
(17 miles/26km)
Chawton, GU34 1SD
☎ 01420 83262

Marwell Zoological Park
(7 miles/11km)
Colden Common, SO21 1JH
☎ 01962 777 407
www.marwell.org.uk

The Watercress Line
(7 miles/11km)
The Railway Station, Alresford, SO24 9JG
www.watercressline.co.uk
Travel by steam or Heritage diesel train through ten miles of beautiful Hampshire countryside between Alresford and Alton stations.

Events
Grange Park Opera
Making Merry
Winchester Hat Fair
(Street Theatre)
Winchester Festival
Winchester Mayfest

Hotels & Dining
Try the Tourist Information Centre, see Essential Contacts for details.

Something Special

Lainston House Hotel
(4 miles/6.5m)

Sparsholt, SO21 2LT
☎ 01962 776 088
www.lainstonhouse.com
A charming 17th century house standing elegantly in sixty-three acres of Hampshire parkland with the longest line of lime trees in England. An award-winning hotel with a delightful restaurant serving produce from its own kitchen garden.

The Winchester Hotel
Worthy Lane, SO23 7AB
☎ 01962 709 988
Boutique-style hotel in the heart of the historic city with facilities including gym, indoor pool, sauna, solarium and jacuzzi.

Chesil Rectory Restaurant
Chesil Street, SO23 0HU
☎ 01962 851 555
www.chesilrectory.co.uk
Exciting innovative French cuisine in the oldest house in Winchester.

Essential Contacts

Tourist Information Centre
Winchester Guildhall, High Street, SO23 9GH.
☎ 01962 840 500

Theatre Royal
Jewry Street, SO23 8SB
☎ 01962 840440
www.theatre-royal-winchester.co.uk

The Screen Cinema
Southgate Street, SO23 9EF
☎ 01962 856 009

Landmark Visitors Guide: The New Forest; ISBN: 9781843062141; £7.50

Windsor, Windsor And Maidenhead

Getting There

By Road

East or West bound M4, J6.

By Rail & Bus

Mainline connections into Windsor & Eaton Central from most parts of the country.

There are national coach/bus services into Windsor; check online for details.

Background Briefing

Historic Windsor grew up around the magnificent castle; it is delightfully situated on the banks of the River Thames, and has many 17th century buildings together with Georgian town houses and Victorian architecture. Perhaps the best way to see the town is by following the heritage walking trail which leads from the castle and crosses the Thames to Eton College. The Guildhall, where Prince Charles married Camilla, was completed in 1690 by Sir Christopher Wren. In 1697 Wren built his family home in Windsor by the Thames; it has now been extended and is a hotel, having delightful views across the river. Cobbled streets in the town, opposite the castle's Henry VIII Gate, have many interesting buildings dating from the 17th century including a house where William Shakespeare is thought to have written 'The Merry Wives of Windsor''. At another it is said that Charles II kept his mistress Nell Gwynne. Park Street has elegant Georgian buildings and leads to the Long Walk in Windsor Great Park with fine views back to the castle. This pleasant walk, along a tree lined avenue, is three miles long from the castle to the copper statue of George III on Snow Hill.

The castle, with its rich history, is a major tourist attraction, being the largest and oldest occupied castle in the world. Visitors should allow at least two hours to see the magnificent state rooms, treasures from the Royal Collection, St George's Chapel, Queen Mary's Doll's House and the castle grounds. While in Windsor you can go to the theatre, see the changing of the Guard, hire a boat or take a cruise on the Thames, walk the Thames path, hop on an open-top bus for a tour, ride in a horse-drawn hackney carriage, shop til you drop or have a relaxing meal. Windsor has a wonderful variety of places to eat including historic pubs and restaurants, Continental-style pavement cafes and traditional tea rooms.

Windsor is blessed with superb shops, from high street retailers and department stores to designer labels, antiques and quaint souvenir shops. On the outskirts of Old Windsor is the Windsor Farm Shop, stocking a range of products from the Royal farms and small local specialist suppliers. Just across the bridge is Eton with its famous college and its High Street with an eclectic range of shops perfect for browsing. In front of the Cockpit Restaurant is a pair of stocks and a Victorian post box; the restaurant contains the remains of the original cock fighting area, a sport prevalent in the 17th and 18th centuries. With so much to offer Windsor is an ideal centre for a short break with attractions within the town and in the surrounding area.

Places to Visit

Windsor Castle

www.royalcollection.org.uk
The history of this splendid building spans almost 1,000 years and a visit here is a rewarding experience. Magnificent state and semi-state apartments can be seen furnished with treasures from the Royal Collection, including paintings by Holbein, Rubens, Van Dyck and Lawrence, fine tapestries and porcelain, sculpture and armour. The beautiful 14th century St George's Chapel is the burial place of ten monarchs, including Henry VIII and Jane Seymour, as well as being the setting for many royal weddings. Queen Mary's Doll's House, one of the world's most famous doll's houses, is a miniature version of a grand Edwardian home. The castle is the favourite weekend home of the Queen and remains a working castle.

The Changing of the Guard

The Guards can be seen as they march up the High Street and into the castle, but to see the 'changing' ceremony you need to pay to go into the castle. The ceremony takes place outside the Guardroom in the Lower Ward of the Castle. To watch the Guards march up the High Street takes only ten minutes; the actual ceremony inside the castle takes about thirty minutes.

Eton College

The college, founded in 1441 by King Henry VI, has educated eighteen former British Prime Ministers including the Duke of Wellington, Walpole, Pitt the Elder, MacMillan and Douglas-Home. The School Dress of a black tailcoat and waistcoat and pin-striped trousers dates

from the 1850s. Fascinating guided tours of the college include the Cloisters, the College Chapel, the oldest classroom in the College and the Museum of Eton Life.

Other Places to Visit

Savill Garden

www.theroyallandscape.co.uk
The garden within Windsor Great Park covers some thirty-five acres, and is considered to be the finest of its type in the northern temperate region of the world. There are wonderful displays of colour all year round and a stunning new visitor centre complete with restaurant and shop.

Legoland

Winkfield Road, Windsor
SL4 4AY
☎ 0871 2222 001
www.legoland.co.uk
Theme park with interactive rides and attractions.

Windsor Great Park

www.thecrownestate.co.uk
5,000 acres of woodland, lakes and gardens.

Attractions Nearby

Cliveden Gardens (NT)

(8.5 miles/14km)
Taplow, Maidenhead, SL6 0JA
☎ 01628 605069
Magnificent formal gardens overlooking the River Thames, once the exclusive haunt of the rich and famous with celebrated parterre and elegant Italianate mansion.

Dorney Court

(3 miles/5km)
Dorney, SL4 6QP
☎ 01628 604638
www.dorneycourt.co.uk
Dorney Court was built in 1440 and has been lived in by the Palmer family for over 400 years. The adjacent 13th century church of

St James, with Norman front and Tudor tower, can also be visited. Check opening times for house but walled garden centre open daily.

Milton's Cottage

(22 miles/34km)
Deanway, Chalfont St Giles,
HP8 4JH
☎ 01494 872313
www.miltonscottage.org
Visit the Grade 1 listed cottage where John Milton lived and completed Paradise Lost.

Osterley Park (NT)

(13 miles/21.5km)
Jersey Road, Isleworth, TW7 4RB

Top – Bottom: Windsor Castle from the long walk; St George's Chapel; Winsor Royal Station at night; Winsor with church steeple in the background

105

☎ 02082 325050

A magnificent neo-classical house with fine Adam interiors, landscaped park, 18th century gardens and farm shop.

Runnymede (NT)

(3 miles/5km)

Three miles southeast of Windsor, the river leaves the Royal Borough at Runnymede, the famous site of the signing of the Magna Carta. A peaceful walk to the top of the hill offers breathtaking views across the Thames Valley.

Thorpe Park

(8 miles/13.5km)
Staines Road, Chertsey,
KT16 8PN
☎ 08704 444466
www.thorpepark.com
Theme park with rides and attractions.

Events

Festival Spring Weekend

The Royal Windsor Horse Show

Windsor Horse Trials

Carriage Driving Championships

Royal Ascot

Cartier Polo

Hotels & Dining

Book through Royal Windsor Information Centre, see Essential Contacts for details.

Something Special

Sir Christopher Wren's House Hotel & Spa

Thames Street, SL4 1PX
☎ 01753 861354
www.sirchristopherwren.co.uk
An elegant 17th century town house, the former family home of Sir Christopher Wren, is located on the bank of the River Thames

between Eton Bridge and Windsor Castle. The Wren's Club and Spa provides beauty treatments and massages. Also on offer are an open-air jacuzzi spa bath, sauna, relaxation room and gym.

Oakley Court

Windsor Road, Water Oakley,
SL4 5UR
☎ 01753 609988
www.oakleycourt.co.uk
Victorian gothic country house set in thirty-five acres of landscaped gardens with lawns that wander gently down to the banks of the River Thames. The Oakleaf Leisure Club has a multi-gym and indoor swimming pool. Also on offer are a sauna, steam room, jacuzzi, 9 hole golf course, two tennis courts and a croquet lawn. The Body Firm is an exclusive beauty salon within Oakley Court providing treatments for both men and women.

Hampton Court Palace – Landmark Trust

East Molesey Surrey
There are two properties, sleeping six and eight. It's about 13 m/21km away, but like Windsor Castle, it is a Royal Palace!

The Waterside Inn

Ferry Road, Bray, SL6 2AT
☎ 01628 620691
www.waterside-inn.co.uk
World-class French cuisine; dine by the Thames in a pretty 16th century village.

Windsor Grill

65 St Leonard's Road, SL4 3BX
☎ 01753 859658
Mouth-watering dishes at Anthony Worral Thompson's restaurant.

Essential Contacts

Royal Windsor Information Centre

Old Booking Hall, Windsor Royal Station

☎ 01753 743900
Accommodation Hotline:
☎ 01753 743907
www.windsor.gov.uk

Ascot Racecourse

High Street, Ascot, SL5 7JX
☎ 0870 727 1234

Royal Windsor Racecourse

Maidenhead Road, SL4 5JJ
☎ 01753 498400

French Brothers Ltd

The Clewer Boathouse, Clewer Court Road, SL4 5JH
☎ 01753 851900
www.frenchbrothers.co.uk
River cruises on the Royal River Thames.

City Sightseeing Open-Top Bus Tours

☎ 01708 866000
Open top bus tours start from outside the Castle, by Queen Victoria Statue.

Orchard Poyle Horse-Drawn Carriages

☎ 07836 766027
www.orchardpoyle.co.uk
Horse-drawn hackney carriages licensed by Royal Borough of Windsor and Maidenhead. The carriages leave from the taxi rank outside the Castle walls for a thirty minute tour through Windsor and down the Long Walk to Home Park or for the one hour tour continuing to the Great Park via the deer park.

Walking Tours

www.windsorwalks.co.uk

Theatre Royal

Thames Street SL4 1PT
☎ 01753 853888
www.theatreroyalwindsor.co.uk

Landmark Publishing gratefully acknowledges The Royal Borough of Windsor & Maidenhead for the use of the images on page 104.
www.windsor.gov.uk

Top – Bottom: Worcester city and the River Severn; City centre shops; River Severn

Getting There

By Road

M6, J6 (south) or J7 (north).

By Rail & Bus

There are mainline services from around the country into either Shrub Hill or Foregate Street stations in Worcester.

There are coach/bus services into Worcester from around the country although you may have to make changes to complete the journey.

Background Briefing

Worcester, located in the heart of England, is a cathedral city, rich in history with enchanting architecture and tranquil riverside walks. It is also a busy market town and is one of the four top shopping centres in the West Midlands, having a huge variety of shops. Explore the city's fascinating history in one of the many museums and discover ancient buildings on a guided walk. The elegant Guildhall in High Street dates from the 18th century and there are timber-framed houses in both New Street and Friar Street. The latter is the most historic street in the city, having the Tudor House, which has sandstone foundations, thought to date back to the 13th century, and 16th century timber framework. Greyfriars with its marvellous medieval interior and Laslett's Almshouses are also in Friar Street, with King Charles House in New Street. King Charles II made his escape through the back door of this house, now a restaurant, after his defeat in the Battle of Worcester in 1651.

The majestic cathedral is situated on the banks of the River Severn where you can walk by the river, take a river cruise or simply sit and watch the world go by. It is easy to walk around Worcester where you will find art galleries, the Royal Worcester Porcelain Visitor centre, military museums, delightful tearooms, street cafes, coffee shops, ancient hostelries and fine restaurants. While in Worcester you could join a ghost walk, go to the races, watch a county cricket match or have a night out at the theatre. Edward Elgar's association with Worcester is commemorated with a statue in the High Street and a visit can be made to the charming cottage where he was born, now a fascinating museum. The city is surrounded by beautiful countryside and there is a wealth of attractions to visit nearby. The delightful town of Malvern is seven miles to the southwest on the A449.

Places to Visit

Royal Worcester Visitor Centre

Severn Street, WR1 2NE
☎ 01905 21247
www.royalworcester.co.uk
Take the opportunity to see skilled artists at work, take the audio tour through the museum, paint your own plate, take the 'Fascinating Facts Trail' and visit the Royal Worcester shop.

The Commandery

Sidbury Street, WR1 2HU
☎ 01905 361822
www.worcestercitymuseums.org.uk
Step inside this ancient building, the site of the Royalist headquarters during the Battle of Worcester in 1651, and discover the intriguing and exciting history of the people who lived here over the centuries. The building has housed a Monastic Hospital, a college for blind boys and a 20th century print works.

Worcester Cathedral

10A College Green, WR1 2LH
01905 21004
www.worcestercathedral.co.uk
This lovely cathedral dates from Norman times and has medieval cloisters, an ancient crypt and chapter house, richly carved misericords and impressive Victorian stained glass. The impressive tombs of King John and Prince Arthur can be found inside the cathedral and wonderful views over the city can be seen from the top of the tower. The composer Edward Elgar lived in Worcester, and the first performance of the *Enigma Variations* took place in the cathedral in 1899.

City Art Gallery & Museum

Foregate Street, WR1 1DT
☎ 01905 25371

The Greyfriars (NT)

Friar Street, WR1 2LZ
☎ 01905 23571
A wealthy merchant's house built in 1480 with a panelled interior full of interesting textiles and furnishings. An archway leads to a beautiful

walled garden.

Tudor House
Friar Street, WR1 2NA
www.tudorhouse.org.uk
Tudor House has had a varied life in the five centuries since it was built. It has been used as a work place for weavers, tailors, bakers, brewers and as lodgings.

Attractions Nearby

Croome Park (NT)
(8.5 miles/13.5km)
Croome D'Abitot, WR8 9DW
☎ 01905 371006
This magnificent landscaped park has been restored to its former glory. It was Capability Brown's first complete landscaped park and has a lakeside garden with islands, bridges and a grotto. There are miles of walks to enjoy in the gardens and parkland.

Droitwich Spa Brine Baths
(7 miles/11.5km)
St. Andrews Road, Droitwich Spa, WR9 8DN
☎ 01905 793446
www.brinebath.co.uk

Elgar Birthplace Museum
(3.5 miles/6km)
Crown East Lane,
Lower Broadheath WR2 6RH
☎ 01905 333224
www.elgarmuseum.org

Spetchley Park Gardens
(3.5 miles/6km)
Spetchley, WR5 1RS
☎ 01453 810303
A thirty acre Victorian paradise with a fantastic collection of plant treasures from all corners of the globe.

Witley Court (EH)
(10.5 miles/16km)
Great Witley, WR6 6JT
☎ 01299 896636
A spectacular ruin with vast gardens, stunning fountains and woodland walks.

Events
City of Worcester Flower Show
Three Choirs Festival
(every 3 years, 2008 and 2011)
Victorian Street Fayre
(Christmas)
Worcester Festival

Hotels & Dining
Try the local Tourist Information Centre, see Essential Contacts for details.

Something Special

The Elms Hotel
(12 miles/19km)
Stockton Road, Abberley, WR6 6AT
☎ 01299 896666
www.theelmshotel.co.uk
A luxury family hotel in an imposing Queen Anne mansion set in gardens and surrounded by beautiful countryside.

Fownes Hotel
City Walls Road, WR1 2AP
☎ 01905 613151
www.fownesgroup.co.uk
A modern hotel in a converted former glove factory and just two minutes walk from the city centre.

Landmark Trust
Shelwick Court, nr Hereford
Approx twenty miles from Worcester, but the house is centred on a medieval great chamber. You may think it worth the journey. Sleeps eight.

King Charles II Restaurant
King Charles House, New Street, WR1 2D
☎ 01905 22449
Mouth-watering dishes in an historic house.

The Quay Restaurant
The Quay, WR1 2JN

Top – Bottom: The Commandery; Worcester has many interesting shops including Durrants; The Guildhall

☎ 01905 745792
www.thequayworcester.co.uk
Quietly situated on the banks of the Severn with wonderful views.

Essential Contacts

Tourist Information
The Guildhall, High Street, WR1 2EY
☎ 01905 726311

Huntingdon Hall and Swan Theatre
Box Office ☎ 01905 611427
www.worcesterlive.co.uk

Worcester Racecourse
Grandstand Road, Pitchcroft, WR1 3EJ
☎ 0870 220 2772
www.worcester-racecourse.co.uk

Worcester River Cruises
37 The Tything, WR1 1JL
☎ 01905 611060

Landmark Visitor Guide: Severn & Avon; £9.99, ISBN 9781843063902

York, North Yorkshire

York Minster

Getting there

By Road

South: A1M to J45/ take A46.
North: A1M to J47/ take A59 (15–20 minute drive from the A1).

By Rail & Bus

Mainline trains call at York Rail Station.

Several coach/bus companies run a service to York Coach Stop.

Background Briefing

Eboracum was the name given to the area settled by the famous ninth Roman Legion in AD71; it was the Vikings who named the town 'Jorvik' from which the name of York is derived. Today, marvellous York is a city of living history best explored on foot; wander along the city streets or saunter through the Shambles to discover a fascinating mix of history and architecture. The iconic York Minster is the largest gothic cathedral in Northern Europe and a visit here is not to be missed. This majestic building is sure to impress, whether admiring the splendid exterior when walking the perimeter, or by stepping into the magnificent interior. Fairfax House is a fine Georgian townhouse; the Merchant Adventurer's Hall is one of the best preserved medieval guildhalls in Europe, and Barley Hall is York's finest medieval townhouse.

Walking the medieval city walls of York, which are almost three miles long and beautifully preserved, will reveal different perspectives of the city. Alternatively, wonderful views can be seen from Clifford's Tower and the Minster or, if you don't want to climb, take a ride on the gigantic observation wheel at the National Railway Museum. York has a choice of world-class museums where you can learn about railways, stroll through a Victorian Street, marvel at archaeological treasures or step back in time to experience life in Viking days. There are art galleries, antique centres, street entertainers, vibrant cafes and a variety of delightful shops. After dark you can see a show, relax in a wine bar, join a ghost walk or simply stroll through the city's dramatic streets. The scenic countryside around York is dotted with castles and stately homes while further afield are the Yorkshire Dales with heather-covered moorland, quiet country lanes, footpaths and picturesque villages.

Places to Visit

Jorvik Viking Centre

Coppergate, YO1 9WT
☎ 01904 543402
www.jorvik-viking-centre.co.uk
Time cars take you back 1,000 years in this award-winning venue, to visit the streets and experience the sights and smells of Viking York.

National Railway Museum

Leeman Road YO26 4XJ
☎ 08448 153139
www.nrm.org.uk
This is the world's largest railway museum with three giant halls full of railway legends. See, among others, the Mallard, the Japanese Bullet train and the Chinese locomotive, one of the largest steam locomotives ever built in Britain. A fascinating attraction for all the family with interactive exhibits and daily demonstrations.

York Castle Museum

☎ 01904 687687
www.yorkcastlemuseum.org.uk
The museum is located in the city's former debtors' prison, where Dick Turpin spent his last night. Nowadays you can walk through the recreated street called Kirkgate and experience the sights and sounds of Victorian Britain.

York Minster Cathedral

www.yorkminster.org
The three superbly proportioned square towers of the largest medieval Gothic cathedral north of the Alps dominate the city. This architectural masterpiece, renowned for its medieval stained glass, provides a wealth of history for you to discover. Don't miss the beautiful choir or the octagonal Chapter House containing some of the Minster's finest carvings, most dating from 1270–80. History comes alive in the Undercroft where an audio tour takes the visitor through Roman, Norman and Viking remains, the jewels of the treasury, and the atmospheric Crypt. Climb to the top of the central tower and gaze across the pinnacles and gargoyles of the Minster, to the streets of historic York and to the countryside beyond.

The North Yorkshire Moors

Top – Bottom: York city clock; Sign post outside of York Mansion House; View of York city showing the famous York Minster in the background

Treasurer's House (NT)
Minster Yard, YO1 7JL
☎ 01904 624247
Town house dating back to medieval times. Carefully restored over a thirty year period.

Other Places to Visit

Barley Hall
2 Coffee Yard, off Stonegate
☎ 01904 610275
www.jorvik-viking-centre.co.uk/barleyhall
Enjoy a hands-on experience at this medieval townhouse.

Clifford's Tower
Tower Street, YO1 9SA
☎ 01904 646940
www.cliffordstower.com
Once the central stronghold of York Castle with wonderful views from the top.

Dig–An Archaeological Adventure
St Saviours Church, St Saviourgate, YO1 8NN
☎ 01904 627097
www.digyork.com
Dig through layers of artificial soil to reveal the secrets of York's past.

Fairfax House
Castlegate, YO1 9RN
☎ 01904 655543
www.fairfaxhouse.co.uk
A stunning 18th century townhouse with a unique collection of furniture, silver ceramics and clocks.

Quilt Museum and Gallery
St Anthony's Hall, Peaseholme Green, Y01 7PR
☎ 01904 613242
Europe's first museum dedicated to quilt making and textile arts.

Mansion House
St Helens Square, YO1 9QN
☎ 01904 552036
Discover the remarkable story of the Lord Mayors of York and their entertainment for the good of the city!

Merchant Adventurers Hall
☎ 01904 654818
One of the world's finest medieval guildhalls.

Roman Bath Museum
St Sampson's Square, Under the Roman Bath Pub.
☎ 07871 561172
The Roman ninth legion's bath house, now below street level.

Yorkshire Air Museum
Halifax Way, Elvington, York, YO41 4AU
☎ 01904 608595
www.yorkshireairmuseum.co.uk
Award-winning museum based on an authentic WWII Bomber Command Station.

York Art Gallery & Yorkshire Museum
Exhibition Square, YO1 7EW
☎ 01904 687687
www.yorkartgallery.org.uk
The gallery has an outstanding collection of British and European art while the museum houses architectural and geological treasure. The museum is set in ten acres of beautiful botanic gardens.

York Maze
Elvington Lane, YO19 5LT
☎ 01904 415364
www.yorkmaze.co.uk
The largest maize maze in the world.

Attractions Nearby

Beningbrough Hall and Gardens (NT)
(8 miles/13km)
Beningbrough, YO30 1DD
☎ 01904 472027
This wonderful Georgian house is filled with 18th century treasures and has beautiful gardens and parkland.

The Gardens themselves are maintained to a high standard with fine features such as a walled garden, Victorian bedding area, rock gardens and heather beds.

Burnby Hall Garden and Museum
(14 miles/23km)
33 The Balk, Pocklington YO42 2QF
☎ 01759 307125
www.burnbyhallgardens.com
Burnby Hall Gardens is home to the National Collection of waterlilies; there are over eighty varieties to

be spotted in the two lakes. The Stewart Collection within the gardens is a unique display of sporting trophies and memorabilia collected by the late Major Stewart.

Castle Howard
(14 miles/23km)
Castle Howard, YO60 7DA
☎ 01653 648333
www.castlehoward.co.uk
Magnificent 18th century house situated in breathtaking parkland, where Brideshead Revisited was filmed.

Selby Abbey
(14 miles/23km)
The Crescent, Selby, YO8 4PU
☎ 01757 703123
www.selbyabbey.org.uk
A wonderful Norman building with 14th century Washington window and a stunning interior.

Sutton Park
(8 miles/13.5km)
Sutton-On-The-Forest,
YO61 1DP
☎ 01347 810249
www.statelyhome.co.uk
Sutton Park is a fine example of early Georgian architecture overlooking beautiful parkland. The house contains beautiful 18th century furniture and paintings.

Hotels & Dining
Book through York Visitor Information Centre, see Essential Contacts for details.

Something Special

Aldwark Manor
Nr Alne YO16 1UF
☎ 01347 838146
www.qhotels.co.uk
This Victorian manor house is set in 120 acres of beautiful countryside, some fourteen miles from York. It has a purpose-built leisure spa with luxurious facilities and treatment rooms.

York Marriott
Tadcaster Road, YO24 1QQ
☎ 01904 701000
www.yorkmarriott.co.uk
This four star hotel, overlooking York racecourse and Knavesmire parkland, has leisure facilities including swimming pool, steam room, sauna, spa bath and gym, The hotel has recently benefited from a £2.5 million development programme.

Landmark Trust
Cawood Castle Gatehouse
Lovely medieval building sleeps 4. About ten miles south of York.

The Blue Bicycle
34 Fossegate
☎ 01904 673990
www.thebluebicycle.com
For something completely different, dine out in this 19th century brothel in one of the original booths or 'beds' overlooking the River Ouse! There is fine food on offer too.

The Lime House
55 Goodramgate
☎ 01904 632734
www.limehouserestaurant-york-.co.uk
Award-winning restaurant with outstanding food served in a relaxed friendly atmosphere.

Events
Contact the Visitor Information Centre for details of festivals held during the year.

The York Festival

Yorvik Viking Festival

Festival of Food and Drink

St Nicholas Fayre

Festival of Angels

Essential Contacts

Visitor Information Centre
De Grey Rooms, Exhibition Square, York, YO1 7HB
☎ 01904 550099
www.visityork.org

Grand Opera House
☎ 0870 6063595
www.GrandOperaHouseYork.org.uk

York Theatre Royal
☎ 01904 623568
www.yorktheatreroyal.co.uk

The Dungeon Tour
☎ 01904 632599
www.thedungeons.com
An evening walking tour in the most haunted city in Europe.

Ghost Hunt of York
☎ 01904 608700
www.ghosthunt.co.uk

The Original Ghost Walk of York
☎ 01759 373090
www.theoriginalghostwalkofyork.co.uk
Leaves Kings Arms Pub nightly at 8pm.

York walking trails
Available from the Visitor Information Centre or online at www.visityork.org/explore

York Boat
☎ 01904 628324
www.yorkboat.co.uk
seventy-five minute cruises with live commentary.

York City Sightseeing
☎ 01904 65558
www.city-sightseeing.com
Open-top bus tours with commentary.

York Pullman Bus Company
☎ 01904 622992
www.yorkpullmanbus.co.uk

York Racecourse
☎ 01904 620911
www.yorkracecourse.co.uk

Photograph acknowledgements

Lindsey Porter: Back Cover right, 5, 14, 15, 39 top left, top right & bottom, 45, 46, 49, 56, 64 top right, middle & bottom, 65, 66 bottom, 52 bottom, 52 top, 67 top, 72, 96 right, 97 right top & right bottom, 101, 107 middle, 108

Chris Gilbert: 40 & 41

Mark Titterton: Back Cover top, 16, 17, 100 top, middle & bottom

Gloucester City Council (www.visitgloucester.info): 48

Harrogate International: 50 & 51

Ipswich Borough Council (www.visit-ipswich.com): 53

www.visitwestnorfolk.com: 54 & 55

Lincoln Tourism (www.visitlincolnshire.com): 7 mini pic, 8 bottom, 24, 25, 59, 60 & 91

Bath Tourism (www.visitbath.co.uk): 19

The Royal Borough of Windsor & Maidenhead (www.www.windsor.gov.uk): 104

Hull & East Yorkshire (VHEY): 22 & 23

Destination Bristol (www.visitbristol.co.uk): Back cover second down, 9 top left, 26

www.visit-suffolk.org.uk: 29, 30 & 31

Yorkshire Dales & Harrogate Tourism (www.yorkshiredales.org): 89

Somerset Tourism Partnership (www.visitsomerset.co.uk): 9 right top, 94 & 95

The images below are courtesy of www.shutterstock.com with copyright to:

Amra Pasic: 42 bottom left. 43 bottom & top, 79 top; *André Klassen:* 109 bottom;
Andrea Seemann: 38 right, top & bottom; *Andresser:* 80 bottom; *Andrew Baker:* 61;
Artur Bogacki: 58 top right & bottom right; *Asher Cheung:* 27 top middle; *Asher Welstead:* 105 top;
B.S Karan: 38 top left; *Bertrand:* 20 bottom; *Bjarne Henning Kuaale:* 42 top right;
Bob Cheung: 27 left, 27 bottom middle; *Bryan Busovick:* 86 top right;
Chad Bontrager: 18 second to bottom & bottom; *Charlie Bishop:* 67 bottom;
Chris Green: 38 bottom, 62 bottom left; *Chris Jonner:* 85 bottom; *Chrislofoto:* 195 bottom;
Christoffer Vika: 75; *Countryroad:* 74 middle & bottom; *Daniel Gale:* 82 bottom;
Darren Pierse Kelly: 76 bottom; *Darren Turner:* Back Cover Bottom, 73; *David Carruthers:* 9 left top
David Hughes: 9 left middle, 93 bottom, 64 top, 66 top, 93 second to bottom & bottom right, 107 top & bottom;
Dhoxax: 6, 32 top *E. Sweet:* 86 left *Edyta Pawlowska:* Back cover third down, 32 bottom;
Gail Johnson: 10, 11, 20 middle & top, 21, 36 second to top, 42 top left, 74 top; *Gary 718:* 93 top right;
George Green: 69, 100 top right; *Guy Erwood:* 77 top, second to top & second to bottom;
Helmut Konrad Watson: 35 middle left & right; *Itinerant Lens:* 77 bottom; *James D. Hay:* 105 second to top;
Jeff Dalton: 39 bottom, 62 bottom right; *John Hemmings:* 62 left top; *Jon le-bon:* 27 right;
Kevin Eaves: 9 bottom right, 42 middle & right; *Kim Pin Tan:* 9 left bottom, 18 top & second to top;
L.L. Chubb: 105 second to bottom; *Lance Bellers:* 13, 35 middle right; *Laurence Gough:* 102, 110 top;
Lee Torrens: 82 top left; *Len Green:* 52 bottom; *Mark William Richardson:* 58 left & middle right;
MARKABOND: 85 top, second to top & second to bottom; *Martin Green:* 99 bottom right;
Matthew Collingwood: 99 tom middle & bottom middle; *Mike J Roberts:* 52 top; *Neil Roy Johnson:* 32 middle;
Paul Cowan: 80 middle; *Paul Reid:* 68, 70; *Peter Guess:* 36 top, second to bottom & bottom, 37, 43 middle;
Philip Lange: 99 left; *Rachelle Burnside:* 35 left; *Richard Bowden:* 76 top;
Ronfromyork: 88, 110 middle & bottom; Front cover *Sandy Maya Matzen:* 57; *Sania:* 80 top;
Stephen Aaron Rees: 96 left, 97 top; *Stephen Meese:* 7 top; *Steve Smith:* 9 right bottom, 100 right bottom; *Susannah Grant:* 86 bottom right; *Tatjana Brila:* 62 bottom right; *Timothy Carge:* 99 top right; *Tom Cummins:* 80 second to top, 82 top right; *Tom Davison:* 79 bottom & second to bottom; *W H Chow:* 62 left middle, 93 second to bottom